641.65 Rip
Ripert, Eric,
Vegetable simple /
$35.00   on1127066050

3 4028 10711 3624
HARRIS COUNTY PUBLIC LIBRARY

W9-BWE-818

BY ERIC RIPERT

VEGETABLE SIMPLE

VEGETABLE SIMPLE

Eric Ripert

PHOTOGRAPHS BY NIGEL PARRY

RANDOM HOUSE · NEW YORK

Copyright © 2020 by Eric Ripert
Photographs © Nigel Parry

All rights reserved.

Published in the United States by Random House, an imprint
and division of Penguin Random House LLC, New York.

RANDOM HOUSE and the HOUSE colophon are registered trademarks
of Penguin Random House LLC.

LIBRARY OF CONGRESS CATALOGING-IN-PUBLICATION DATA
Names: Ripert, Eric, author. | Parry, Nigel, photographer.
Title: Vegetable simple / Eric Ripert ; photographs by Nigel Parry.
Description: New York : Random House, [2020] | Includes index.
Identifiers: LCCN 2019050133 (print) | LCCN 2019050134 (ebook) |
ISBN 9780593132487 (hardcover) | ISBN 9780593132494 (ebook)
Subjects: LCSH: Cooking (Vegetables) | LCGFT: Cookbooks.
Classification: LCC TX801 .R587 2020 (print) |
LCC TX801 (ebook) | DDC 641.6/5—dc23
LC record available at https://lccn.loc.gov/2019050133
LC ebook record available at https://lccn.loc.gov/2019050134

Printed in China on acid-free paper
randomhousebooks.com

2 4 6 8 9 7 5 3 1
First Edition

Book design by Debbie Glasserman

TO THE WELL-BEING OF ALL

INTRODUCTION

It may seem a bit strange to start a cookbook devoted to vegetables by saying that I have been drawn to fish as long as I have been in kitchens. But from age fifteen, when I started culinary school, to my training with Joël Robuchon in Paris to my nearly three decades as chef of Le Bernardin in New York City, my entire career has been about seafood. Fish is incredibly delicate and requires a great deal of focus, technical skill, and experience to prepare in a way that enhances, rather than hides, its essential qualities. It was Gilbert Le Coze, self-trained chef and master of seafood (and my mentor in the early days of Le Bernardin), who first showed me the beauty of cooking seafood with a light touch and a lot of respect.

Over the years, we have developed a mantra at Le Bernardin: "The fish is the star of the plate." And while that remains true, I have recently started to wonder why we weren't highlighting vegetables in the same way, with the same level of care. In 2014, we opened a wine bar next to the restaurant and created a menu consisting largely of small, shareable vegetable-based dishes. Inspired by that process, we introduced a vegetable tasting menu at Le Bernardin two years later. While my passion for seafood has not waned, it has started to become obvious to me over these past years that my focus is widening to include vegetables as a central ingredient—not only in my life as a chef, but also as an enthusiastic eater. This shift has been subtle, at times even unconscious, but once I realized how important vegetables had become to my cooking and to my diet, I decided I had to write *Vegetable Simple*.

When I sat down and began to create this book, the realization dawned that the book had actually been inside me for a long time. It started, in fact, with my earliest experiences: dishes from my childhood, the kitchens of my mother and grandmothers, the gardens of my grandfathers, my yearlong sabbatical on a farm after my military service, and, more recently, the recipes I have found myself reaching for again and again when entertaining guests or cooking for my family. Looking back at my own relationship with food, I see vegetables have been hard-wired in me from an early age. Nothing thrilled me as a child more than trips to the market with my grandmother to find the perfect ingredients for ratatouille, or our adventures in my grandfather's modest but painstakingly tended garden plot, where he proudly grew lettuces, radishes, string beans, potatoes, and anything else he could. I would spend hours up in the boughs of an apricot tree watching my grandmother and aunts through the kitchen window as they prepared soup with the tomatoes and summer squash we'd picked that morning. My diet during these summers spent with family in Provence consisted mostly of vegetables, with fish on Fridays and meat on Sundays. Back in Andorra, my mother, who is an excellent cook, would prepare elaborate three-course meals that always included vegetable dishes like potato gratin and morels à la crème.

When I cook vegetables today, my goal is to showcase their natural flavors and qualities, so simplicity is key. Keeping the recipes in this book easy and uncomplicated allows me to serve a variety of them at once with minimal effort. I rarely go into dinner parties with a preconceived idea of what I'm going to cook; instead, I like to be inspired by whatever looks good and is in season at the market or farmstand. Hosting friends on the weekends is a huge part of my life, and my goal is to feed them well and to bring a sense of fun to the table. I make five or six of these vegetable recipes and arrange all the dishes in the center of the table so everyone can serve themselves family style, or I set up a buffet and encourage my guests to take a bit of everything. Food naturally brings people together, and it makes me so happy to use my experience as a chef to gather everyone around the table to share a meal that I took great pleasure in preparing for them. I always take a second to appreciate that moment after everyone has been seated and raised their glasses in a toast, when my guests start to pass dishes to one another, filling their plates and taking their first bites.

When thinking about how I wanted to structure this book, I approached it in the same way as my trips to the market: with freedom. While the recipes are set out in a loose natural progression from starters to dessert, I want people to have fun with this book, to flip through the pages and be inspired to try any one or two (or three) dishes at a time, rather than feel the need to adhere to strict categories of appetizers, mains, and sides. I get real pleasure out of spending a whole afternoon or even a full day in the kitchen, but I realize not everyone is able to do that, so I have included recipes that come together in less than an hour for a quick and easy meal. I have also included a basic guideline to shopping, storing, cleaning, and making the most out of your vegetables because I believe that good cooking begins at the source, and there are several important steps in the process before you begin your work in the kitchen.

There's a broad spectrum of recipes in the book, from dips and snacks to appetizers, soups, and salads, to pastas and grains, as well as many dishes that could stand alone as main courses. Most of the recipes serve four, so if you are having a light lunch with friends, for example, you might want to try only one or two recipes, but if you are serving dinner for a larger group, I recommend preparing a variety of dishes and serving them family style. Grilled Corn Elote Style, Coleslaw, Herbes de Provence–Crusted Tomatoes, Potato Tortilla Española, and Frosé would make a wonderful summer spread, while a feast for the colder months could be made up of Butternut Squash, Ginger, Turmeric Soup; Slow-Roasted Cauliflower; Rutabaga Gratin; and Mushroom Bolognese.

I'm not a pastry chef, but I do have a sweet tooth, so I couldn't write this book without including some of my favorite easy-to-make desserts, like Chocolate Mousse and Sticky Toffee Puddings, as well as some drinks that take you from breakfast to an afternoon pick-me-up to celebrating with friends.

The approach to cooking and eating reflected in these pages has become a central part of how I live. As I do with fish, I like to pay homage to vegetables and prepare them in a way that enhances their best qualities. I want them to shine, I want to bring out their brightness and beauty. This book, then, is an expression of my evolution not only as a chef, but also as a home cook who loves food and entertaining.

Vegetable cooking has become a growing trend in recent years, not only among chefs, but also among the wider food community and home cooks looking to incorporate healthy changes to their diet. I personally have found that I feel good after eating vegetable-rich dishes—and that feeling stays with me. Naturally, I want to feel good again after my next meal. It's a positive cycle that I want to pay forward with *Vegetable Simple*. We're only starting to discover just how beneficial eating vegetables as a main food source can be to our own well-being and the health of the planet, not to mention the positive impact on sustainability, as well as on the welfare of animals.

My intention is not to convert you to a vegetarian or vegan diet or to impose any judgment on your eating habits, but to inspire you to cook and enjoy delicious, simply prepared vegetables knowing that, ultimately, this benefits the well-being of all.

POPCORN, YUZU-CITRUS SALT

SERVES 4

Popcorn purists may want to make this the traditional way with oil and a pan, but I find the microwaveable kind easier, less messy, and just as tasty. Popcorn is super versatile and can be seasoned with a whole range of flavors such as grated parmesan, truffle oil, or dried herbs and spices. Here I add yuzu and citrus for an unexpected bright twist.

1 bag (about 3 ounces) unsalted microwave popcorn

1 teaspoon yuzu salt

1 teaspoon shichimi togarashi

Finely grated zest of 1 lemon

Finely grated zest of 1 lime

POP THE POPCORN in the microwave according to the package directions.

Toss the hot popcorn with the yuzu salt, togarashi, and citrus zests and serve immediately.

SPICY PLANTAIN CHIPS

SERVES 4 TO 6

Canola or another neutral oil
(about 2 cups), for frying

6 to 8 large green plantains

Fine sea salt and chili powder

SPECIAL EQUIPMENT

Mandoline

Deep-fry/candy thermometer

Ultimate crispiness is the key here. I recommend eating these the same day you make them, but if you are planning to make a big batch, make sure you store any leftovers in a dry space in a tightly sealed container. They will last a couple of days. Take extra care when using a mandoline, as the blades are extremely sharp. If your mandoline does not have a hand guard, I recommend you wear a Kevlar glove.

POUR 4 INCHES OF OIL into a tall-sided, heavy-bottomed pot and heat the oil over medium-high heat to about 300°F.

Line a sheet pan or large plate with paper towels. Peel the plantains. Using a mandoline, slice them into pieces approximately ⅛ inch thick. The plantains can be cut widthwise into coins, or lengthwise into strips.

Working in batches (to avoid overcrowding), carefully lower the plantains into the pot. Stir the plantains more or less constantly, so that they cook evenly. Once the bubbles have dissipated and the chips begin to brown, use a slotted spoon to remove them from the oil and transfer to the paper towels to drain. Season the chips right away with salt and chili powder to taste.

Let the chips dry and crisp up for about 15 minutes, then serve.

TOASTED COCONUT

SERVES 6

There are many ways to break down a coconut . . . my trick to keep things simple for this recipe is to buy one already out of its shell and in pieces—a common shelf item in grocery stores these days. If you do plan on splitting the coconut yourself, make sure you do it over a bowl or some other vessel to catch the liquid. When toasted, these chips are best eaten immediately, as they go soggy quickly.

1 coconut, whole or already out of its shell

Fine sea salt

PREHEAT THE OVEN TO 375°F.

If using a whole coconut, examine the coconut and locate the ridge that runs across it. Wrap the coconut in a kitchen towel with the ridge side up. Over a bowl or vessel, hit the coconut with a mallet until it breaks. Reserve any liquid for another use.

Place the coconut on a sheet pan, flesh side down, and bake in the oven for 10 minutes to loosen the flesh from the shell. (Leave the oven on.) When the coconut is cool enough to handle, use a butter knife to remove the flesh. If there is any skin on the coconut, remove it with a vegetable peeler.

Using a mandoline, carefully shave the coconut flesh into very thin strips.

Line the sheet pan with parchment paper and distribute the shaved coconut on it in an even layer. Season lightly with salt.

Bake for 4 minutes. Remove from the oven, shake the pan slightly, and return to the oven to bake until golden brown, another 2 to 3 minutes. Serve warm or at room temperature. Store leftovers in an airtight container.

SPECIAL EQUIPMENT

Mallet

Mandoline

Parchment paper

CARAMELIZED WALNUTS

SERVES 6

¼ cup light corn syrup

½ cup sugar

Red pepper flakes or cayenne pepper

Fine sea salt

3 cups walnuts

SPECIAL EQUIPMENT

Silicone baking mat or parchment paper

Spicy and sweet, with a great texture, these are the ultimate snack. Pecans work well, too, if you prefer. I make them in big batches and store them in jars in a very dry place where they will last a few days. They also make a wonderful gift.

PREHEAT THE OVEN TO 300°F. Line a sheet pan with a silicone baking mat or parchment paper.

In a large saucepot, combine the corn syrup, sugar, and 1 tablespoon water and heat over medium heat, stirring constantly, until the sugar is melted, about 3 minutes. Add a pinch each of pepper flakes and salt. Add the walnuts and stir to completely coat.

Transfer the nuts to the lined sheet pan, spreading them in an even layer.

Bake until the nuts are golden brown, 8 to 12 minutes. Remove from the oven, let cool to room temperature, and store in an airtight container.

MARINATED OLIVES

SERVES 4

Choosing a good mix of varieties, flavors, and colors adds complexity and texture, and they look great, too. I find pitted are best so that you can enjoy them without the extra work. If you don't have a mason jar, a tightly sealed container of similar size will do. These will keep in the refrigerator for weeks, and the bonus is they get better the longer you leave them.

IN A BOWL, combine the olives, garlic, rosemary, and lemon zest. Add the olive oil and vinegar and gently toss to combine. Cover and refrigerate for at least 12 hours before serving.

Serve chilled or at room temperature.

2 cups mixed pitted olives, such as Niçoise, Picholine, and Castelvetrano

1 garlic clove, halved

1 sprig rosemary

1 strip lemon zest, thinly sliced

3 tablespoons extra-virgin olive oil

1 tablespoon sherry vinegar

HUMMUS

SERVES 4 TO 6

2 cups dried chickpeas
(or 6 cups canned, drained
and rinsed)

Salt

½ cup tahini

¼ cup plus 1 tablespoon
extra-virgin olive oil

2 garlic cloves, peeled

¼ cup fresh lemon juice
(from 1 large lemon)

Freshly ground white pepper

2 teaspoons paprika

SPECIAL EQUIPMENT

Food processor

There are two options here: Use dry chickpeas and soak them overnight, or buy good quality canned or jarred ones. Either way, serve the hummus with warm pita or crudités, or even use it as a sandwich spread. If you wish, you can garnish it with nuts, chopped olives, pomegranate seeds, or herbs like fresh parsley.

IF USING DRIED CHICKPEAS, soak them in water to cover by 2 inches for 12 hours or overnight in the refrigerator. Drain them and transfer to a large pot. Add cold water to cover the beans by 2 inches and add 2 teaspoons salt. Bring the water to a simmer and cook until the beans are tender, about 50 minutes. They should be tender and cooked through, but not waterlogged. Reserving the cooking broth, drain the chickpeas.

In a food processor, combine the tahini, ¼ cup of the extra-virgin olive oil, the garlic, and the chickpeas and blend until smooth. Add the lemon juice and salt and white pepper to taste, and thin the consistency as desired with some of the reserved chickpea cooking liquid, or warm water if using canned beans.

Scrape the hummus into a bowl, sprinkle with the paprika, and drizzle the remaining 1 tablespoon of olive oil on top.

BABA GANOUSH

SERVES 4

The beauty of baba ganoush is its versatility. Though a light spread, it's silky with a rich texture and tons of flavor. Serve with pita, vegetables, or crackers.

PREHEAT THE OVEN TO 350°F.

Season the flesh side of each eggplant half with salt and pepper and drizzle each half with 1 tablespoon of the oil. Place each half flesh side down on a sheet pan and bake until the flesh is slightly browned and very soft, 25 to 30 minutes.

When the eggplant is cool enough to handle, use a spoon to scoop the flesh into a blender (discard the skin). Add the garlic, cumin, and lemon juice and blend on medium speed. With the machine running, slowly drizzle in the remaining 2 tablespoons olive oil.

Scrape the mixture into a bowl and season with salt and white pepper. Serve the baba ganoush with a bit of cumin sprinkled over it and olive oil drizzled on top.

1 medium eggplant (about 1½ pounds), halved lengthwise

Fine sea salt and freshly ground white pepper

4 tablespoons extra-virgin olive oil, plus more for drizzling

1 small garlic clove, peeled

½ teaspoon ground cumin, toasted, plus more for serving

1 teaspoon fresh lemon juice

SPECIAL EQUIPMENT

Blender

CAPONATA TOAST

SERVES 4

2 tablespoons extra-virgin olive oil

½ medium onion, cut into ¼-inch dice

1 rib celery, cut into ¼-inch dice

2 garlic cloves, finely chopped

1 red bell pepper, cut into ¼-inch dice

1 medium eggplant, cut into ¼-inch dice

Fine sea salt and freshly ground white pepper

1 tomato, peeled, seeded, and cut into ¼-inch dice

1 tablespoon red wine vinegar

1 tablespoon small brined capers

1 tablespoon finely chopped fresh parsley

1 baguette, cut into 16 slices (½ inch thick) and toasted

To me, caponata toast feels like a sophisticated version of bruschetta, with more complex flavors. A platter of these makes an impressive passed canapé or even a centerpiece on the table for guests to help themselves. Top the toasts with the eggplant at the last minute to avoid them getting soggy. Here I use baguette, but any type of bread or even crackers will do.

IN A LARGE, HEAVY-BOTTOMED POT, heat the olive oil over medium heat. Add the onion and celery and cook until softened, about 5 minutes. Stir in the garlic, bell pepper, and eggplant, season with salt and pepper, and cook, stirring regularly, until tender, about 15 minutes.

Add the tomato and vinegar and cook until the tomatoes soften and release their juices, about 4 minutes. Remove from the heat and stir in the capers and parsley. Season to taste with salt and white pepper. Top the baguette slices with caponata and serve immediately.

TAPENADE

SERVES 4

I love this dip, and I often serve it alongside hummus and baba ganoush for the perfect dip trifecta. If you don't have a mortar and pestle, use a knife or coarsely chop in a food processor.

THOROUGHLY RINSE THE OLIVES under cold water.

In a large mortar or the bowl of a food processor, combine the olives, garlic, parsley, lemon juice, and olive oil. If using a mortar and pestle, hold the mortar with your nondominant hand. With the pestle in your other hand, gently push and twist until a coarse paste is formed. If using a food processor, pulse mixture until the same coarse texture is achieved.

Transfer to a bowl and serve.

2 cups mixed pitted olives, such as Niçoise, Picholine, and Castelvetrano

1 small garlic clove, peeled

1 tablespoon chopped fresh parsley

1 tablespoon fresh lemon juice

3 tablespoons extra-virgin olive oil

SPECIAL EQUIPMENT

Large mortar and pestle or food processor

FLASH-CURED CUCUMBERS

SERVES 4 TO 6

1 cup kosher salt

8 Japanese cucumbers

I learned this technique on one of my first trips to Japan. I was amazed at the difference in taste and texture between a cucumber that was rolled in salt and one that wasn't. For some reason the salt not only enhances the flavor tremendously, but also gives it a firmer texture. I like to use Japanese cucumbers, as they are smaller and a perfect size for snacking. They are commonly found in grocery stores or Asian markets.

PLACE HALF THE SALT IN A SHALLOW PAN large enough to hold the cucumbers in a single layer.

Roll each cucumber in the salt, pressing down slightly so that the salt adheres to the skin. Arrange the cucumbers in the pan and cover with the remaining salt. Let rest for 2 to 3 minutes.

Remove the cucumbers from the pan and brush the salt off the outside. Slice and serve.

CRUDITÉS

In spring and summer in Provence, it's very common to have an assortment of fresh seasonal vegetables on tables throughout the region, usually presented in traditional bowls made of cork. Serving crudités is a festive way to welcome your guests and makes a colorful centerpiece, as well. Use vegetables at their peak, and serve with one or more dips.

WASH ALL VEGETABLES very well and dry on a kitchen towel. Cut any combination of these vegetables—whatever is best and in season—into attractive shapes and arrange on a platter.

Serve with tapenade, hummus, or baba ganoush.

½ cup broccoli florets

½ cup cauliflower florets

½ cup trimmed and quartered radishes

2 Persian (mini) cucumbers, cut into spears

3 ribs celery, halved lengthwise and cut into 3-inch pieces

4 small carrots, peeled and halved lengthwise

1 head Belgian endive, root end trimmed off, separated into leaves

12 cherry tomatoes

6 asparagus spears, peeled from the tip down and cut into 4-inch pieces

16 green beans, ends trimmed

1 small zucchini, cut into spears

Hummus (page 14), Baba Ganoush (page 17), or Tapenade (page 21), for serving

"AIGO BOULIDO" BROTH

SERVES 4

9 garlic cloves, smashed and peeled

12 large fresh sage leaves

2 tablespoons extra-virgin olive oil, plus more for drizzling

8 slices (¼ inch thick) baguette

Fine sea salt and freshly ground white pepper

½ cup grated Gruyère cheese (optional)

Sometimes referred to as garlic soup, this typical Provençal broth was traditionally a favorite of farmers and laborers who extolled its health virtues, such as aiding digestion and curing hangovers. Don't be fooled by the seemingly stark ingredients—this broth is impressively rich, and loaded with flavor. My grandfather often made this, and it quickly became one of my favorite soups as a child.

PREHEAT THE OVEN TO 350°F.

In a medium pot, combine 6 cups water, 8 of the garlic cloves, and the sage and bring to a simmer. Let cook at a simmer for 5 minutes, then remove from the heat and add the olive oil and let sit for 5 minutes to infuse.

Meanwhile, arrange the bread slices on a baking sheet. Rub one side of each slice with the remaining garlic clove, and drizzle with some olive oil. Season to taste with salt and white pepper. Top each with 1 tablespoon of the Gruyère (if using) and transfer the sheet to the oven to toast the bread until golden brown, 3 to 5 minutes.

Strain the broth, place 2 toasts in each of four bowls, divide the broth evenly, and serve immediately.

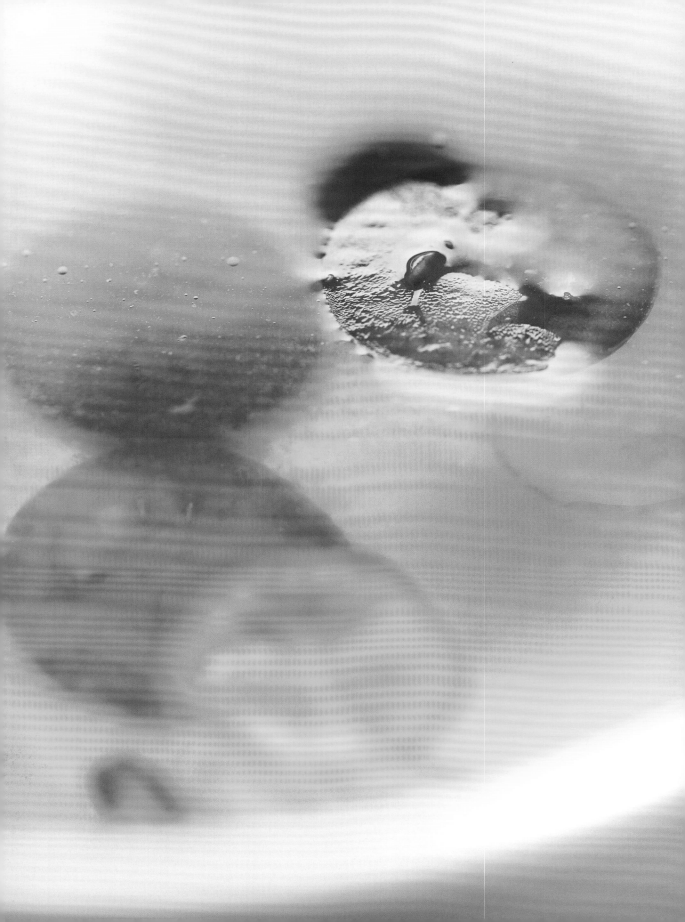

END OF SUMMER TOMATO "TEA"

SERVES 4

While light and refined, this "tea" gets its depth and complexity from good-quality tomatoes. I like to make this light starter at the end of summer or the beginning of fall, when tomatoes are at their peak.

WORKING IN BATCHES, place the chopped tomatoes in a blender and pulse to form a fine puree. Line a fine-mesh sieve with two layers of cheesecloth and place it over a large bowl. Transfer the tomato puree to the sieve and let drain at least 2 to 3 hours, or overnight in the refrigerator, to yield about 6 cups of clear tomato water. Reserve 1 cup of the drained tomato pulp and set it aside. (Save any leftover pulp for another use, perhaps in a sauce or as a base for a spread or dip.)

In a small sauté pan, heat the olive oil over medium heat. Add the shallot and garlic, reduce the heat to low, and cook until it is soft and translucent but not browned, about 2 minutes. Stir in the reserved tomato pulp and cook the mixture until it is nearly dry. Season this tomato jam with salt and white pepper and set aside.

Transfer the tomato water to a small pot and bring it to a simmer, skimming off and discarding any foam. Season the water with salt and white pepper to taste and set aside, keeping it hot.

Toast the baguette slices until golden brown, either in an oven at 400°F or in a toaster. Spread each toast with a thin layer of tomato jam.

Add the sliced cherry tomatoes and scallion to the hot tomato water and divide it evenly among four warmed bowls. Serve with 2 slices of toast on the side per person.

14 large beefsteak tomatoes, coarsely chopped

1 tablespoon extra-virgin olive oil

1 tablespoon finely chopped shallot (about ½ small)

1 garlic clove, finely chopped

Fine sea salt and freshly ground white pepper

1 small baguette, cut on the diagonal into 8 slices (¼ inch thick)

5 cherry tomatoes, varying colors, very thinly sliced

1 scallion, very thinly sliced

SPECIAL EQUIPMENT

Blender

Fine-mesh sieve

Cheesecloth

MUSHROOM CONSOMMÉ

SERVES 4

3 pounds button mushrooms

Fine sea salt and freshly ground white pepper

I like to serve this consommé at the beginning of a meal. The lightness is deceptive and it surprises my guests with its rich and intense flavor. You can use the strained mushrooms again by incorporating them into another dish or simply enjoy them marinated in olive oil and a splash of vinegar, seasoned with salt and pepper.

SET ASIDE 4 WHOLE MUSHROOMS. Place the rest of the mushrooms in a medium pot and add 4 quarts of water. Bring to a boil, reduce to a simmer, and cook for 3 hours.

Strain the liquid through a sieve into a clean bowl, pressing on the mushrooms to release any liquid that has been absorbed. You should have 6 cups of liquid. If there is more than that, return the liquid to the pot and bring to a boil to reduce to 6 cups.

Slice the reserved mushrooms, add to the consommé, and bring to a simmer. Remove the consommé from the heat, season with salt and white pepper to taste, and serve immediately.

SWEET PEA SOUP

SERVES 4

Frozen peas work well for this, as the peas are harvested and frozen at their peak, before they mature and become starchy. I always keep a bag in the freezer, which allows me to make this soup year-round. Serve warm on cold days and cold on warm days.

IN A SMALL BOWL, mix 2 tablespoons of crème fraîche and the chopped mint, season with salt and white pepper, cover, and refrigerate.

In a medium pot, bring 2½ cups of water to a boil and add 1 teaspoon salt. Add the peas—if using fresh, cook them for 3 to 4 minutes; if frozen, blanch them for 2 to 3 minutes.

Remove the pot from the heat and transfer the mixture to a blender. Puree on high speed until smooth. Once the mixture is smooth, add the butter (if using) and blend until it is incorporated. Taste the soup and season with salt and white pepper.

Divide the soup evenly among four bowls. Garnish each serving with ½ tablespoon of crème fraîche and serve immediately.

4 tablespoons crème fraîche

1 tablespoon finely chopped fresh mint

Fine sea salt

3 cups shelled green peas (12 ounces), fresh or frozen

2 tablespoons unsalted butter (optional)

Freshly ground white pepper

SPECIAL EQUIPMENT

Blender

SILKY BROCCOLI SOUP

SERVES 4

1 large or 2 small stalks broccoli, florets separated and stems thinly sliced

Fine sea salt

2 tablespoons unsalted butter

Freshly ground white pepper

Often people discard the broccoli stems and only use the florets, but I like to use both. This soup can be made in advance and keeps in the fridge for a couple of days. You can top it with toasted croutons for garnish and texture.

IN A MEDIUM TO LARGE POT, bring 3 cups of water to a boil. Add 1 teaspoon salt, then add the broccoli stems and cook until they start to soften, about 2 minutes. Add the florets and cook until tender, about 5 minutes.

SPECIAL EQUIPMENT

Blender

Once the florets and stems are tender, drain them in a sieve set over a bowl, reserving the liquid. Transfer the broccoli to a blender, adding enough of the reserved liquid to cover. Add the butter and puree until very smooth. You can adjust the consistency with more of the reserved cooking water if it's too thick.

Taste the soup and adjust the seasoning with salt and white pepper. Serve in four warmed bowls, or chill immediately and reheat later, to keep the soup's bright green color.

TOMATO, SUMMER SQUASH SOUP

SERVES 4

The tomatoes concentrate during the cooking process, giving them a full, intensified flavor. This is a wonderfully versatile soup that can be served hot or chilled like gazpacho.

IN A MEDIUM SAUCEPAN, warm 2 tablespoons of the olive oil over medium heat. Add the onion and garlic and sweat for 2 minutes. Add the tomatoes, season lightly with salt, and cook for 5 minutes. Add enough water to just cover the tomatoes (about 2 cups) and cook for another 10 minutes.

Remove the pot from the heat and transfer the mixture to a blender. Puree until very smooth. Taste and season with salt and white pepper.

In a sauté pan, warm the remaining 2 tablespoons olive oil over medium heat. Add the bell pepper and sweat until slightly softened, about 1 minute, before seasoning with a bit of salt. Add the zucchini and eggplant and cook until tender, another 5 to 7 minutes. Taste the vegetables and adjust the seasoning as needed.

Divide the bell pepper, zucchini, and eggplant mixture evenly among four soup bowls. Pour the hot tomato soup over, garnish each serving with chopped basil leaves, drizzle olive oil on top, and serve.

4 tablespoons extra-virgin olive oil, plus more for drizzling

½ cup diced red onion (⅓ to ½ medium)

1 garlic clove, thinly sliced

4 large beefsteak tomatoes, coarsely chopped

Fine sea salt and freshly ground white pepper

½ cup diced red bell pepper

½ cup diced zucchini

½ cup diced eggplant

12 small fresh basil leaves, chopped

SPECIAL EQUIPMENT
Blender

BABY LEEK, POTATO SOUP

SERVES 4

4 tablespoons (½ stick)
unsalted butter

4 baby leeks, trimmed and
medium diced

1 pound Yukon Gold potatoes
(about 2½ inches in diameter),
peeled, medium diced, and
held in water

Fine sea salt and freshly
ground white pepper

SPECIAL EQUIPMENT

Blender

Served cold, this is a classic vichyssoise. However, I actually prefer it hot, as the harmonious flavors become even more enhanced when heated.

IN A MEDIUM POT, melt the butter over low heat. Add the leeks and sweat them until slightly softened, about 3 minutes. Drain the potatoes and add them to the pot along with 4 cups of water. Bring the mixture to a simmer and cook until the potatoes are just tender, 20 to 25 minutes.

Drain the vegetables in a sieve set over a bowl, reserving the cooking liquid. Set aside one-quarter of the vegetables for serving. Transfer the remaining vegetables to a blender and puree together until smooth. Be careful not to overblend it, as the starch in the potatoes can turn it into a gooey paste. Taste the soup and season with salt and white pepper. If the soup is too thick, adjust the consistency to your liking with a splash or two of the reserved cooking water.

Divide the reserved vegetables for garnish among four warm bowls. Ladle the soup over and serve immediately.

CELERY ROOT SOUP

SERVES 4

Easy to prepare, this inexpensive soup brings big dividends in terms of flavor and presentation. Celery root (celeriac) is unjustly underrated, maybe because of its aesthetic, which is why I like to serve this soup in a hollowed-out celery root to showcase the whole vegetable. It's striking and impressive.

4 large celery roots

1½ cups whole milk

2 tablespoons unsalted butter

Fine sea salt and freshly ground white pepper

PREHEAT THE OVEN TO 400°F.

Place the celery roots in a large baking dish about as deep as the vegetables are tall. Add ½ inch water to the dish, cover it tightly with foil, and bake until the celery roots are easily pierced with the tip of a paring knife, about 1 hour. Remove from the oven and allow to cool.

Use a sharp knife to slice 1 inch off the top of each root. Then, using a small spoon, remove as much flesh as possible without piercing the sides. Place the flesh in a medium-large pot, and reserve the hollowed-out celery roots separately.

Add the milk, 1½ cups water, and butter to the pot with the celery root flesh. Bring to a simmer over medium heat, then transfer to a blender and puree until smooth. Taste and season with salt and white pepper, divide the soup among the warm hollowed-out celery roots, and serve.

SPECIAL EQUIPMENT
Blender

BUTTERNUT SQUASH, GINGER, TURMERIC SOUP

1 large butternut squash, peeled, seeded, and chopped (about 5 cups)

1 tablespoon chopped peeled fresh ginger (from a 1-inch piece)

1 teaspoon ground turmeric, plus more for finishing

4 tablespoons (½ stick) unsalted butter

Fine sea salt and freshly ground white pepper

SPECIAL EQUIPMENT

Blender

Once late fall arrives, I make this soup often. You can substitute pumpkin or another similar squash such as acorn or delicata for the butternut squash. The ginger brings a spiciness and heat while the turmeric gives it a beautiful, cheerful yellow color. The anti-inflammatory properties of both ginger and turmeric make this a perfect feel-good soup. It may not be quite medicinal, but it comes pretty close.

IN A LARGE POT, combine the squash, ginger, turmeric, butter, and salt and white pepper to taste. Add water to cover the squash by 1 inch (about 3 cups). Bring the mixture to a simmer and cook until the squash is completely tender, 15 to 20 minutes. Remove from the heat.

Transfer the mixture to a blender and puree until smooth, taste the soup, and adjust the seasoning with salt and white pepper if necessary.

Serve the soup in warmed bowls, garnished with a sprinkle of turmeric.

BUTTER LETTUCE SALAD

SERVES 4

Working with whole heads of lettuce here brings a nice aesthetic to the salad. Your guests will enjoy cutting into the lettuce head with a knife and fork, as they would a wedge salad. The crunchy texture and sweeter flavor of the heart balance the softer, more savory leaves.

IN A SMALL BOWL, combine the sherry vinegar, balsamic vinegar, and salt and white pepper to taste. Slowly whisk in the olive oil.

Season the lettuce lightly with salt and white pepper. Using a pastry brush, paint each lettuce leaf with the vinaigrette. Sprinkle with the herb mixture. Quarter and serve immediately, on chilled plates.

2 teaspoons aged
sherry vinegar

2 teaspoons balsamic vinegar

Fine sea salt and freshly
ground white pepper

2 tablespoons extra-virgin
olive oil

1 large head butter lettuce,
washed and patted dry
(it's important to clean the
lettuce thoroughly of soil and
sand), core trimmed but head
left whole

2 teaspoons finely chopped
fresh tarragon leaves

2 teaspoons finely
chopped chives

SPECIAL EQUIPMENT

Pastry brush

AVOCADO SALAD

SERVES 4

4 firm-ripe avocadoes, pitted, peeled, and cut lengthwise into wedges

Fine sea salt and freshly ground white pepper

1 small red onion, very thinly sliced

6 cherry tomatoes, very thinly sliced

½ small jalapeño pepper, very thinly sliced

2 tablespoons fresh cilantro leaves

1 lime, cut into 4 wedges

Extra-virgin olive oil

This has all the elements of a good guacamole while maintaining the texture of each ingredient. The avocado should be slightly firm, not too hard and not too soft. Serve and eat this salad straightaway, as avocado oxidizes quickly. You can also serve it with some tortillas or toast alongside.

ARRANGE THE PIECES OF 1 AVOCADO on each of four chilled plates and season each with salt and white pepper.

In a bowl, gently toss together the onion, tomatoes, jalapeño, and cilantro leaves, and season with salt and white pepper. Divide this salad mixture evenly among the four plates on top of the avocado.

Squeeze a lime wedge over each salad, drizzle with olive oil, and serve.

ENDIVE BLUE CHEESE SALAD

SERVES 4

Hands down, one of my all-time favorite salads. It's so easy to make, and easy to eat—no knives or forks, just your hands! I recommend a sharp, not-too-creamy blue cheese—more like a Roquefort than a Gorgonzola, but to each their own. The dressing can last quite a while if kept refrigerated.

MEASURE OUT AND SET ASIDE about 1 tablespoon cheese for garnish. Place the remaining cheese in a food processor along with the crème fraîche, and keep the milk close at hand. Pulse the cheese and crème fraîche together while drizzling in the milk. Take care not to over-mix; you want a dressing with a somewhat chunky texture. Add the lemon juice, then season with salt and pepper.

On each of four plates, arrange the endive leaves in a spoke pattern, with the points facing out. Spoon the dressing into the center of the plates, garnish with the reserved blue cheese, and serve.

½ cup crumbled blue cheese (2½ ounces), at room temperature

½ cup crème fraîche

¼ cup whole milk

1 tablespoon fresh lemon juice

Fine sea salt and freshly ground black pepper

4 large heads Belgian endive, root end trimmed off, separated into individual leaves

SPECIAL EQUIPMENT

Food processor

WATERMELON "PIZZA"

SERVES 4

4 crosswise slices (1 inch thick) whole seedless watermelon, each slice cut into quarters, thin green outer layer of skin removed

Fine sea salt and freshly ground white pepper

1 cup crumbled feta cheese (about 5 ounces)

⅓ cup quartered pitted green olives (about 2 ounces)

⅓ cup quartered pitted black olives (about 2 ounces)

30 small mint leaves or 2 tablespoons chopped mint

Great for adults and kids alike! I love the combined flavors of the sweetness of the melon with the saltiness of the feta and brininess of the olives. I prefer to use seedless yellow watermelons, as they are generally sweeter and can offer more contrast, not to mention the gorgeous color.

LAY THE WATERMELON SLICES on a serving platter and lightly season them with salt and white pepper. Scatter the feta, olives, and mint on each slice to resemble pizza and serve immediately.

MELON "AU PORTO"

When in season, this melon dish is served throughout France on special occasions, and very often on Sundays. If you don't have a melon baller, you can cut the fruit into cubes. The idea is to have small bites. Eat with a spoon, never a fork, so you can eat the melon and drink the port at the same time. A simple and perfect pairing.

2 cantaloupes, halved and seeded

1 cup good-quality port

USE A MELON BALLER to turn the melon flesh into as many balls as possible. If not serving right away, refrigerate the melon balls in a covered bowl.

When ready to serve, divide the melon balls among four chilled bowls. Pour ¼ cup port over each bowl and serve.

SPECIAL EQUIPMENT

Melon baller

COLESLAW

SERVES 8

1 head green cabbage (about 2½ pounds), quartered, cored, and very thinly sliced

1 large carrot, grated

6 scallions, thinly sliced

3 tablespoons finely chopped fresh tarragon

½ cup mayonnaise

3 tablespoons red wine vinegar

3 tablespoons sugar

Fine sea salt and freshly ground black pepper

Coleslaw is a barbecue staple, but I like to serve it all summer long and even through fall and winter when I add some shredded apple. You need a sharp knife as well as good cutting skills for this recipe, or you can use a food processor if you prefer. It's best served very cold and keeps well in the refrigerator. Leftover slaw makes a great sandwich condiment, or even its own sandwich filling between the bread of your choice.

IN A LARGE BOWL, combine the cabbage, carrot, scallions, and tarragon and toss gently.

In a separate bowl, combine the mayonnaise, vinegar, sugar, and salt and pepper to taste. Stir or whisk until well combined.

Pour the dressing over the cabbage and mix well. Taste a piece of cabbage and adjust the seasoning if necessary. Refrigerate for at least 1 hour.

Note: It may seem that the coleslaw is scantily dressed, but after at least 1 hour, covered, in the refrigerator, the salt and sugar in the dressing will draw some of the moisture out of the cabbage and carrot, making this a juicier salad.

COUSCOUS TABBOULEH

SERVES 4

There are many variations of tabbouleh, but this version is my favorite, as it's not *too* herbaceous. This is a substantial dish, and when entertaining I often serve it alongside other lighter salads, dips, and accompaniments.

Fine sea salt

1½ cups couscous

2 Persian (mini) cucumbers, diced

2 beefsteak tomatoes, seeded and diced

Freshly ground white pepper

2 tablespoons finely chopped fresh parsley leaves

2 tablespoons finely chopped fresh mint leaves

2 tablespoons fresh lemon juice

¼ cup extra-virgin olive oil

IN A MEDIUM SAUCEPOT, bring 1½ cups of water to a boil and add a pinch of salt. Stir in the couscous, remove from the heat, cover, and let stand for 5 minutes. Fluff the couscous with a fork, place in a large bowl, and set aside to cool completely.

In a large bowl, combine the cucumbers, tomatoes, and salt and white pepper to taste. Toss well and let sit for 5 minutes. To serve, fold the couscous into the vegetable mixture. Add the parsley, mint, and lemon juice. Slowly add the olive oil, mixing gently, and serve.

GRATED CARROT SALAD

SERVES 4

2 large carrots, each about 10 inches in length

Fine sea salt and freshly ground white pepper

Juice of 1 lemon

3 tablespoons extra-virgin olive oil

SPECIAL EQUIPMENT

Box grater

This salad has it all: It's super simple, super healthy, and super tasty. The lemon and olive oil bring out the sweetness of the carrots. Use large, good-quality carrots, as they will be easier to grate. Growing up, I was told that eating carrots puts you in a good mood and I think this salad proves that there's some truth to that.

USING THE LARGE HOLES ON A BOX GRATER, shred the carrots and transfer to a bowl. Season the carrots with salt and white pepper, then add the lemon juice and oil and toss well. Taste and adjust the seasoning if needed.

QUINOA, BABY SPINACH SALAD

SERVES 4

Quinoa is a light, tasty grain with richness and depth. This salad is excellent in summer when squash and tomatoes are plentiful and at their peak. It's well balanced and can be a complete meal on its own or as an appetizer or side. Once cooked, quinoa also keeps well in the fridge.

IN A MEDIUM SAUCEPAN, combine the quinoa and 1½ cups of water and bring to a boil over medium-high heat. Add a pinch of salt, cover the pot, reduce the heat, and let the quinoa simmer until the water has cooked out, 10 to 12 minutes. Remove from the heat and let it sit for 5 minutes, then fluff with a fork or spoon. Set aside to cool.

In a large bowl, combine the zucchini, yellow squash, cucumber, and tomatoes. Season lightly with salt and white pepper and set aside.

In a small bowl, whisk together the mustard, lemon juice, and a pinch of salt, then whisk in the canola oil, thinning with a splash of water if necessary.

In a second large bowl, dress the spinach with half the vinaigrette. Divide the leaves among four plates. Fold the quinoa into the diced vegetables, then gently toss with the remaining vinaigrette. Divide the quinoa mixture evenly among the plates of dressed spinach and serve immediately.

1 cup quinoa, rinsed and drained

Fine sea salt

1 cup large-diced zucchini

1 cup large-diced yellow squash

1 Persian (mini) cucumber, cut into large dice

16 cherry tomatoes, halved

Freshly ground white pepper

1 teaspoon Dijon mustard

1½ tablespoons fresh lemon juice

¼ cup canola oil

4 cups baby spinach, rinsed and patted dry

SHAVED FENNEL, PARMESAN SALAD

SERVES 4

1 bulb fennel, trimmed
(fronds reserved)

Fine sea salt and freshly
ground white pepper

1 tablespoon extra-virgin
olive oil

1½ teaspoons fresh lemon juice

½ cup freshly shaved
parmesan cheese (about
2 ounces)

SPECIAL EQUIPMENT

Mandoline

Fennel and parmesan make for a clean, beautiful, and un-complicated salad. Fennel can oxidize quickly, so I recommend shaving it at the last minute for optimum texture as well as to keep its fresh, anise aroma.

USING A MANDOLINE, thinly shave fennel from root to top into a bowl. Season the fennel with salt and white pepper. Add the oil and lemon juice and gently toss to coat. Divide among four plates, garnish with shaved parmesan and a few fennel fronds, and serve immediately.

ISRAELI COUSCOUS SALAD

SERVES 4

Different from regular couscous, Israeli couscous (sometimes called pearl couscous) has a pasta-like consistency. Bursting with bright colors and flavors, this salad should be served chilled and is a real crowd pleaser for family-style meals.

FILL A SOUP POT with 3 quarts of water, bring to a boil, and season with salt. Add the couscous and cook until tender, about 8 minutes. Drain the couscous, transfer to a bowl, and toss with 2 tablespoons of the olive oil. Spread the couscous out on a sheet pan and refrigerate till cool.

Set up a large bowl of ice and water. In a second soup pot of boiling salted water, blanch the mint, basil, and cilantro for 30 seconds. Drain and shock in the ice water until cool. Gently squeeze out the herbs in a clean kitchen towel to remove excess water.

In a blender, combine the blanched herbs and yogurt and puree until very smooth.

In a bowl, combine the couscous, cucumbers, tomato, lemon juice, salt and white pepper to taste, and the remaining 2 tablespoons olive oil and gently toss. Fold in the yogurt mixture to coat the couscous and vegetables. Serve chilled or at room temperature.

Fine sea salt

2 cups Israeli couscous

4 tablespoons extra-virgin olive oil

¼ cup loosely packed fresh mint leaves

¼ cup loosely packed fresh basil leaves

¼ cup loosely packed fresh cilantro leaves

½ cup Greek yogurt

2 Persian (mini) cucumbers, cut into small dice

1 medium beefsteak tomato, seeded and cut into small dice

Juice of 1 lemon

Freshly ground white pepper

SPECIAL EQUIPMENT

Blender

SNAP PEA SALAD

SERVES 4

Fine sea salt

1 pound sugar snap peas, strings removed

¼ cup buttermilk

1 tablespoon Greek yogurt

Finely grated zest of ½ lemon

1 tablespoon extra-virgin olive oil

Freshly ground white pepper

1 cup young pea shoots

¼ cup shaved Pecorino Romano cheese (about 1 ounce)

I make this salad, packed with flavor and light as can be, most often at the beginning of spring when snap peas are at their most tender. I love the contrast of the sweetness of the peas with the sharpness of the cheese.

SET UP A LARGE BOWL OF ICE AND WATER. In a pot, bring 4 quarts of water to a boil and season with salt. Blanch the peas in the boiling water until tender and bright green, 3 to 4 minutes. Drain and plunge into the ice water. Once cool, drain and transfer to a bowl.

In a small bowl, whisk together the buttermilk, yogurt, lemon zest, and olive oil. Taste and season with salt and white pepper.

In another bowl, toss together the peas, pea shoots, and dressing. Taste and adjust seasoning, then divide among four plates. Garnish with the shaved Pecorino and serve immediately.

FAVA BEAN, MINT SALAD

SERVES 4

As with snap peas, I like favas at the start of spring when they are small, tender, and not too starchy. Shelling the beans takes time and involves a few steps. First remove the beans from their pods, then with a paring knife score the beans to remove the skin. Removing the beans from the skin before cooking helps keep their vibrant green color. Cooking beans with skin on gives them a dull gray hue. If you're not in a rush, this can be an exercise in mindfulness.

Fine sea salt

3 cups peeled, shelled fava beans

3 tablespoons sliced almonds

2 tablespoons extra-virgin olive oil, plus more to taste

2 teaspoons fresh lemon juice

Freshly ground white pepper

1 tablespoon thinly sliced fresh mint leaves

¼ cup shaved Manchego cheese (about 1 ounce)

SET UP A LARGE BOWL of ice and water. In a medium pot, bring 2 quarts of water to a boil and season with salt. Add the fava beans to the boiling water and cook for 1 to 2 minutes, until tender, then drain and transfer them to the ice bath. When cool, drain and transfer to a bowl.

Preheat the oven (or a toaster oven) to 350°F.

Arrange the almonds in a single layer on a sheet pan (or toaster oven tray) and toast until lightly browned, 3 to 4 minutes. Transfer to a plate and season lightly with salt.

Add the almonds to the beans, then drizzle in the olive oil and toss. Add the lemon juice and gently toss again. Season with salt and white pepper. Divide the beans among four bowls or plates, garnish with the mint and Manchego, and serve immediately.

ROASTED BELL PEPPER SALAD

SERVES 4

3 red bell peppers

3 yellow bell peppers

1 red onion, thinly sliced

1 teaspoon grated lemon zest

¼ cup red wine vinegar

1 tablespoon small
brined capers

¼ cup extra-virgin olive oil

4 sprigs parsley, leaves only

4 sprigs thyme, leaves only

Fine sea salt and freshly
ground black pepper

SPECIAL EQUIPMENT

Charcoal/gas grill or wire rack

Tongs

There are several ways to remove the skin of the peppers: You can char them over an open flame, fry them in oil, or even bake them. I like the open flame method, as it gives the peppers some smokiness and depth. I prepare this salad a couple of days in advance and keep it in the fridge to let all the flavors come together.

ON A CHARCOAL OR GAS GRILL, or a wire rack over an open flame, dry-roast each bell pepper until the skin is charred and black, turning them with tongs to get all sides evenly cooked, about 5 minutes. Keep a big bowl nearby and place each cooked pepper in it as you go, keeping them covered with plastic wrap.

Let the peppers sit for about 5 minutes, then use a clean kitchen towel or paper towel to wipe away the charred black skins. Cut the top off each pepper and remove and discard the seeds and core inside. Cut each pepper into ½-inch-wide strips.

In a clean bowl, combine the pepper strips, onion, lemon zest, vinegar, capers, and olive oil and toss gently to combine. Fold in the herbs and season with salt and pepper. Serve at room temperature.

CHICKPEA SALAD

SERVES 4

As with the hummus recipe, if you want to make this even quicker and simpler, you can use good-quality canned or jarred chickpeas. I'm a purist, so if I have the time I soak dried chickpeas overnight before cooking them the next day. It's a slightly longer process but it feels good to put in the effort.

PLACE THE CHICKPEAS IN A BOWL and add water to cover by 2 inches. Let soak, refrigerated, for 8 hours or overnight.

Drain the chickpeas and transfer them to a medium pot, along with the garlic, bay leaf, and 1 teaspoon salt. Add water to cover by 2 inches, bring to a simmer, and cook for 50 minutes, until tender.

Drain the chickpeas and transfer to a bowl (discard the garlic and bay leaf). Let the chickpeas cool for a few minutes, then add the vinegar and onion. Let stand for 5 minutes, then fold in the olive oil.

Stir in the parsley, adjust the seasoning with salt and white pepper, and serve.

1 cup dried chickpeas

1 garlic clove, peeled

1 bay leaf

Fine sea salt

2 tablespoons red wine vinegar

3 tablespoons finely diced red onion

2 tablespoons extra-virgin olive oil

2 tablespoons finely chopped fresh parsley

Freshly ground white pepper

ZUCCHINI LINGUINE

SERVES 4

4 medium zucchinis

Fine sea salt and freshly
ground white pepper

1 cup coarsely chopped
fresh mint leaves

Extra-virgin olive oil

SPECIAL EQUIPMENT

Mandoline or vegetable
spiralizer

A mandoline is the best way to re-create the linguine shape, but as always, take extra care when you're using it, and slow down once you've reached the halfway point of slicing each zucchini. The entire salad takes only minutes to prepare, but it's best to make it at the last minute so that the zucchini keeps a firm texture.

IF USING A MANDOLINE, carefully shave the zucchini, with the large teeth setting at a ¼-inch thickness, into a bowl, or spiralize with spiralizer. Season the zucchini linguine with salt and white pepper and place in a colander set over a bowl. Refrigerate for 10 minutes.

Transfer the zucchini to a bowl, add the mint and olive oil to taste, and gently toss. Taste and adjust the seasoning with salt and white pepper, and serve.

ROMAINE CAESAR GRATIN

SERVES 4

Inspired by my dear friend Laurent Manrique, this is a clever play on a Caesar salad. The obvious difference is that the romaine is served quartered and broiled for the gratin effect, but it keeps its crunchiness and freshness. Enjoy straightaway before the romaine wilts or gets soggy.

IN A BLENDER, combine the yolks, garlic, mustard, and lemon juice and puree at medium speed while slowly drizzling in the olive oil, until it is fully incorporated and the dressing resembles a thick mayonnaise. Taste and season with salt. (This dressing will keep in the refrigerator up to 3 days.)

Preheat the broiler or oven to 500°F.

Lay out the romaine halves, cut side up, on a sheet pan large enough to hold them in a single layer. Brush each half with some of the dressing, making sure that it gets between the leaves. Cover each romaine half with parmesan and bake or broil until the cheese is bubbling and golden brown, 3 to 4 minutes. Finish with a pinch of pepper and serve immediately.

2 egg yolks

1 garlic clove, sliced

1 tablespoon Dijon mustard

3 tablespoons fresh lemon juice

½ cup extra-virgin olive oil

Fine sea salt

4 jumbo romaine lettuce hearts, halved lengthwise and trimmed

2 cups freshly grated parmesan cheese (about 8 ounces)

Freshly ground black pepper

SPECIAL EQUIPMENT
Blender

Pastry brush

WARM POTATO, GOAT CHEESE PARFAITS

SERVES 4

4 large Yukon Gold potatoes

¼ cup Niçoise olives, pitted and chopped

¼ cup Picholine olives, pitted and chopped

2 tablespoons red wine vinegar

2 tablespoons plus 1 teaspoon sherry vinegar

¼ cup plus 1 tablespoon extra-virgin olive oil

Fine sea salt and freshly ground white pepper

8 ounces goat cheese

¼ cup milk, as needed

2 cups arugula

SPECIAL EQUIPMENT

Parchment paper

Four 3-inch ring molds

Kitchen torch (optional)

Not everyone has a kitchen torch, but you can get almost the same effect in the broiler. The warm goat cheese marries well with the briny olives and potato. I cook potatoes with the skin on to retain their flavor. They are easier to peel when warm, just be careful not to burn your fingers. I recommend serving with some toast.

IN A LARGE POT, cover the potatoes with water and season with salt. Bring to a boil and cook the potatoes until easily pierced in the thickest part with a paring knife, about 30 minutes. Remove the potatoes from the hot water and let cool slightly, but peel the potatoes while still quite warm and transfer to a large bowl.

Preheat the oven or toaster oven to 500°F.

Coarsely mash the potatoes. Add the chopped olives and mix them in. In a small bowl, combine the red wine vinegar and 2 tablespoons of the sherry vinegar. Fold the vinegar into the potato mixture, then fold in ¼ cup of the oil. Taste and season with salt and white pepper.

Place the goat cheese in a bowl and add a splash of milk at a time to thin it to the consistency of thick paste.

Line a sheet pan or toaster oven tray with parchment. Place four 3-inch ring molds on the pan and fill each three-quarters full with the potato mixture. Top with goat cheese. Transfer the sheet pan to the broiler or toaster oven to bake until just warm, 3 to 4 minutes. If using a torch, torch the tops of the goat cheese until it begins to caramelize.

Place the arugula in a bowl and toss with the remaining 1 teaspoon sherry vinegar and 1 tablespoon olive oil. Season with salt and white pepper.

Transfer a parfait to each of four serving plates and remove the ring mold. Garnish with the dressed arugula and serve immediately.

FLUFFY BASMATI RICE

SERVES 4

Long-grain basmati rice is fragile and can be difficult to make fluffy if you don't know the proper technique. I learned it from Persian friends and it's much simpler than you would expect. The result is that the rice is so tasty and light it practically dissolves in your mouth. I find this amount of rice to be the right quantity for a side dish for four guests.

1½ cups basmati rice

1½ tablespoons unsalted butter

½ teaspoon fine sea salt

PLACE THE RICE IN A MEDIUM BOWL and wash with cold water. Repeat one or two more times, until the water runs clear.

Transfer the rice to a medium pot and add 3 cups of water, the butter, and the salt. Stir gently, then bring the mixture to a boil. Reduce the heat to a simmer, cover the pot with a tight-fitting lid, and cook until the rice is tender, about 15 minutes.

Remove the pot from the heat and let it sit, covered, for 5 minutes. Fluff the rice with a fork and serve.

HERB FALAFEL

SERVES 4

FALAFEL

2 cups dried chickpeas

4 scallions, finely chopped

2 garlic cloves, chopped

¼ cup chopped fresh
parsley leaves

1 tablespoon chopped fresh
mint leaves

1 teaspoon finely chopped mild
green chile pepper

1½ teaspoons ground cumin

1 teaspoon ground coriander

1 teaspoon fine sea salt

1½ teaspoons baking powder

Canola oil (3 to 4 cups), for
deep-frying

YOGURT DIPPING SAUCE

½ cup plain yogurt

3 tablespoons tahini

2 teaspoons fresh lemon juice

Fine sea salt and freshly
ground white pepper

SPECIAL EQUIPMENT

Food processor

Deep-fry/candy thermometer

I love the texture of these falafel; they're moist and light, even though they're deep-fried. The mint is delicate, not overpowering, and gives them an airy freshness. If making the quenelles is a challenge (it takes practice), you can roll the falafel by hand into pieces the size of golf balls or use an ice-cream scoop.

MAKE THE FALAFEL: Place the chickpeas in a bowl and add water to cover by 2 inches. Refrigerate and soak for 12 hours.

Drain the chickpeas and place them in a food processor, along with the scallions, garlic, parsley, mint, chile, cumin, coriander, and salt. In a small bowl, combine the baking powder and 1 tablespoon warm water and add to the food processor. Process until smooth, then transfer to a bowl. Cover and refrigerate for 30 minutes.

Make the yogurt sauce: In a bowl, stir together the yogurt, tahini, lemon juice, and salt and white pepper to taste. Set aside.

Pour 3 inches of oil into a heavy-bottomed pot and heat to 375°F on a deep-fry thermometer.

Divide the falafel mixture into 16 equal portions and gently roll into balls; or form quenelles by transferring the mixture back and forth between two spoons until it forms a smooth, oval shape.

Line a sheet pan with paper towels and keep it nearby. Working in batches (to avoid overcrowding), fry the falafel balls in the oil until golden brown, 4 to 5 minutes. Remove from the oil with a slotted spoon and transfer to the paper towels to drain.

Serve with yogurt dipping sauce.

VIDALIA ONION RISOTTO

SERVES 6

Onion risotto may sound a little plain, but it's anything but. The onions bring sweetness, richness, and lightness all at once. White wine provides just the right amount of acidity for balance, and if you wish you can finely grate some lemon zest at the end.

3 tablespoons canola oil

1 medium Vidalia onion, finely diced

Fine sea salt and freshly ground white pepper

½ cup dry white wine

2 cups Arborio rice (about 16 ounces)

½ cup finely grated parmesan cheese (about 2 ounces)

3 tablespoons unsalted butter

IN A LARGE SAUTÉ PAN, heat 2 tablespoons of the canola oil over medium heat. Add the onion, reduce the heat to medium-low, and cook, stirring occasionally, until caramelized, 15 to 20 minutes. Remove from the pan, season with salt and white pepper, and set aside.

In two separate saucepans, bring the wine and 4 cups water to a simmer.

In a Dutch oven, heat the remaining 1 tablespoon canola oil over medium heat. Add the rice and toast it in the oil for 2 minutes, stirring regularly. Stir in the wine, then ½ cup of water, reduce the heat to medium-low, and cook, stirring, until the liquid has almost been absorbed. Repeat this three times, using 1 cup of water each time.

Stir in the onion and a final ½ cup of water and bring to a simmer. Slowly stir in the parmesan, adding a bit more water if the risotto is too thick or the rice isn't yet tender. Beat the butter into the risotto until incorporated, season with salt and white pepper, and serve.

CHILI

SERVES 4

½ cup dried black beans (or a 16-ounce can, drained and rinsed)

½ cup dried red beans (or a 16-ounce can, drained and rinsed)

Fine sea salt

2 teaspoons canola oil

1 medium yellow onion, diced

2 red bell peppers, diced

½ jalapeño pepper, seeded and finely chopped

18 button mushrooms, quartered

1 tablespoon chili powder

1 tablespoon freshly ground black pepper

1 teaspoon ground cumin

8 Roma (plum) tomatoes, peeled and crushed (or 12 ounces canned peeled tomatoes)

1 cup shredded cheddar cheese (optional)

½ cup sour cream (optional)

Beans from a can work just as well to make this chili that's full of complex flavors and aromatics. It's satisfying and warming, so I like to make it in late fall when the weather starts to turn. Adding mushrooms replaces the texture of meat and brings an earthy and intense richness.

IF USING DRIED BEANS, place the black and red beans in separate bowls and add water to cover by 2 inches. Let soak, refrigerated, for 8 hours or overnight. Drain the beans, transfer them to two separate pots, and add water to each to cover beans by 2 inches. Bring to a simmer over medium heat, cover, and cook the beans until completely tender, about 1 hour. Season with salt and set aside.

In a large, heavy-bottomed pot, heat the canola oil over medium heat. Add the onion, bell peppers, jalapeño, and mushrooms. Season lightly with salt and sauté until soft, about 5 minutes. Add the chili powder, black pepper, and cumin and cook for another 2 minutes.

Add the tomatoes and bring to a simmer, then add the beans and 1½ cups of water and simmer for 15 minutes more.

Transfer one-third of the chili to a blender and puree until smooth. Stir the puree back into the chili and simmer 5 minutes. Divide among four bowls. If desired, serve with cheddar and sour cream.

SPECIAL EQUIPMENT

Blender

BRAISED LENTILS

SERVES 4

This is easy comfort food for those long winter nights. I use le Puy green lentils for their size and refined flavor, but you can use any lentils you wish. There's a misconception that lentils need to be soaked overnight before cooking, but you're fine to just cook them straight out of the bag after rinsing.

IN A SAUCEPOT, combine the lentils, shallots, carrots, celery, and garlic and cover with 1 inch of water. Add the thyme and bay leaf and cook at a low simmer until the lentils and vegetables are tender, about 1 hour.

Discard the bay leaf and thyme sprigs, season the lentils and vegetables with salt and pepper, and divide among four bowls. Serve hot.

1 cup French green (le Puy) lentils, rinsed

4 small shallots, peeled and halved

2 medium or 1 large carrot, cut into 2-inch lengths

1 rib celery, cut into 2-inch lengths

1 garlic clove, finely chopped

3 sprigs thyme

1 bay leaf

Fine sea salt and freshly ground black pepper

CHEESE POLENTA

SERVES 4

4 cups whole milk

1 teaspoon fine sea salt, plus more to taste

1 cup fine polenta

3 tablespoons unsalted butter

⅓ cup grated parmesan cheese (about 1.5 ounces)

Fine polenta takes about 25 minutes to cook and instant polenta takes 3 or so minutes. While not as rich or dense, the instant version is pretty good if you're short on time. I like the texture to be very soft, and I cook the polenta with milk for added richness. I use butter, too, but if you wish, you can swap in a splash of (extra-virgin) olive oil at the end.

IN A LARGE POT, combine the milk and 3 cups of water and bring to a boil. Stir in the salt. Slowly whisk in the polenta and continue to whisk until the mixture begins to bubble slightly. Reduce the heat to low and cook, stirring frequently, until the polenta is soft, about 25 minutes.

Fold in the butter and parmesan. Taste and adjust the seasoning with salt as desired. Serve hot.

COLD BASIL PASTA SALAD

SERVES 4

Basil is one of my absolute favorite herbs and I love making any dish where it's a main ingredient. The smell brings me right back to summers in Provence and the markets I would visit with my grandma in the mornings. I use Spinosi tagliatelle (you can buy it online), as it cooks quickly, in about 3 minutes, and is light and not at all starchy.

SET UP A LARGE BOWL of ice and water. In a medium pot, bring 2 quarts of water to a boil. Season the water with salt and add the basil leaves. Cook for 30 seconds, then drain the basil and plunge it into the ice bath to stop it from cooking. Once cooled, drain the basil.

In a blender, combine the blanched basil, garlic, and parmesan. With the machine on low speed, slowly drizzle in ½ cup of the oil and continue to blend until it is incorporated. Season the mixture with salt and white pepper to taste. Store in an airtight container until ready to use.

Bring a medium to large pot of water to a boil. Add a large pinch of salt, add the tagliatelle, and cook to al dente, according to the package directions. Drain, then run under cold water to cool. Transfer the pasta to a large bowl and toss it with the pesto and remaining 1 tablespoon of oil.

Divide the pasta among four bowls and serve, topped with additional parmesan if desired.

Fine sea salt

2 cups loosely packed fresh basil leaves (about 1 large bunch)

2 small garlic cloves, finely chopped

½ cup grated parmesan cheese (about 2 ounces), plus more (optional) for serving

½ cup plus 1 tablespoon extra-virgin olive oil

Freshly ground white pepper

12 ounces tagliatelle pasta

SPECIAL EQUIPMENT
Blender

SPAGHETTI POMODORO

SERVES 4

6 large tomatoes, cored

Fine sea salt

12 ounces spaghetti

3 tablespoons extra-virgin olive oil

1 garlic clove

Freshly ground white pepper

4 large basil leaves, torn by hand

Good-quality, uncomplicated ingredients make this one of the easiest pasta dishes to put together at the last minute. The sauce is light and pairs perfectly with spaghetti, though you can use other pasta shapes if you wish. I make this in late summer or early fall with the last of the season's tomatoes.

SET UP A LARGE BOWL of ice and water. Bring a large pot of water to a boil. Add the tomatoes and cook for 30 to 40 seconds to loosen the skins. Scoop out the tomatoes and shock them in the ice bath. When they are chilled, peel the tomatoes and halve them horizontally. Squeeze the tomatoes to remove the seeds and cut the flesh into ¼-inch dice.

Bring a large pot of water to a boil. Add a large pinch of salt, add the spaghetti, and cook to al dente, according to the package directions.

Meanwhile, in a large sauté pan, heat the oil over medium heat. Add the garlic and cook, stirring frequently, for 1 minute. Add the tomatoes and season with salt and white pepper. Stir well and cook at a simmer until the tomato liquid is evaporated, 4 to 5 minutes.

Drain the pasta and add it to the tomato sauce. Toss and cook for 2 minutes. Taste the sauce and adjust the seasoning if desired. Serve in four warmed bowls, garnished with basil.

STEAMED VEGETABLE DUMPLINGS

MAKES 20 DUMPLINGS

These dumplings are fluffy and full of flavor from the ginger and shiitake mushrooms. Buying premade wonton wrappers helps simplify the process; the thinner the wrapper, the more delicate the dumpling.

IN A LARGE SAUTÉ PAN, heat the canola oil over medium heat. Add the onion and cook over medium-low heat until it begins to soften but not brown, 2 to 3 minutes.

Add the ginger, shiitakes, cabbage, carrots, and salt and white pepper to taste. Stir well and cook over medium heat until the vegetables become soft, wilted, and fragrant, about 5 minutes. Remove from the heat and stir in the scallions, cilantro, and sesame oil. Set aside to cool.

Fill a small bowl with warm water. Line a sheet pan or large plate with plastic wrap, waxed paper, or parchment. Place one wonton wrapper on a clean cutting board and place 1 tablespoon of the cooked vegetables in the center. Wet the edge of the wonton wrapper, using a finger dipped into the water, then fold the wrapper over the filling to form a half-moon shape. Press the edges together to seal. Transfer the dumpling to the lined sheet pan. Repeat with the remaining wrappers and filling. Cover the dumplings and refrigerate until ready to cook.

Set up a steamer on your stovetop and steam the dumplings until the wrappers are tender and translucent, about 10 minutes. (If you do not have a steamer, bring a pot of salted water to a boil and cook the dumplings in it for about 5 minutes.)

Plate the dumplings and serve with soy sauce for dipping and lime wedges alongside.

2 tablespoons canola oil

1 cup finely chopped white onion

1 tablespoon grated peeled fresh ginger

2 cups thinly sliced shiitake mushrooms

2 cups thinly sliced napa cabbage

1 cup coarsely grated carrot

Fine sea salt and freshly ground white pepper

¼ cup thinly sliced scallions

¼ cup coarsely chopped fresh cilantro

1 teaspoon sesame oil

20 round wonton wrappers

Best-quality soy sauce, for serving

2 limes, cut into wedges, for serving

SPECIAL EQUIPMENT

Steamer

MUSHROOM BOLOGNESE

SERVES 4

2 tablespoons extra-virgin olive oil

1 shallot, finely chopped

1 garlic clove, finely chopped

4 cups whole button mushrooms, ground or pulsed in a food processor

3 maitake mushrooms, ground or pulsed in a food processor (about 1½ loosely packed cups)

Fine sea salt and freshly ground white pepper

1 cup red wine, reduced to ¼ cup

16 ounces canned tomatoes, pureed in a food processor

1 teaspoon Sriracha sauce

12 ounces tagliatelle

½ cup freshly grated parmesan cheese (optional)

SPECIAL EQUIPMENT

Food processor

Some evenings, there is nothing more satisfying than a warm bowl of Bolognese. The flavor and texture of this recipe rivals that of "real Bolognese" and is much lighter, therefore allows second (and third!) helpings.

IN A MEDIUM POT, heat the olive oil over medium heat. Add the shallot and garlic, reduce the heat to low, and sweat the vegetables for 2 to 3 minutes.

Add the mushrooms and stir well. Increase the heat to medium-high and season the mixture with salt and white pepper. Cook for 3 to 4 minutes, until the mushroom liquid releases and begins to reduce.

Add the reduced wine and cook until the mixture is nearly dry. Add the tomatoes, reduce the heat to a simmer, and cook for 30 minutes, stirring occasionally. Add the Sriracha. Adjust the seasoning with salt and white pepper to taste, cover, and keep warm while you cook the tagliatelle.

Bring a large pot of water to a boil. Add a large pinch of salt, add the tagliatelle, and cook to al dente, according to the package directions.

Drain the pasta and divide it among four warmed bowls. Ladle the sauce over each portion of pasta and serve. If desired, garnish with parmesan.

VEGETABLE LASAGNA

SERVES 4

Re-creating traditional lasagna sheets with zucchini makes this vegetable lasagna even lighter. You'll need a "vegetable sheet cutter" (an attachment for a stand mixer) to slice the zucchini into long, thin sheets (like lasagna sheets), or you could also use a large mandoline (and, as always, be careful). I recommend cutting the baked lasagna with a very sharp knife to serve clean, even portions.

PREHEAT THE OVEN TO 250°F. Line a sheet pan with parchment paper. Arrange the tomatoes, cut side up, on the pan. Season the tomatoes with salt and white pepper and drizzle with the olive oil. Roast in the oven until slightly caramelized and reduced in size by half, about 2 hours. Remove the tomatoes and increase the oven temperature to 375°F. When the tomatoes are cool enough to handle, coarsely chop.

In a large sauté pan, heat the canola oil over medium-high heat. Add the spinach, season lightly with salt, and sauté for 2 minutes. Add the garlic and cook until the liquid has evaporated, about 3 minutes. Transfer to a bowl to cool.

Using a vegetable sheet cutter or a large mandoline, slice the zucchini into thin sheets. Line a cutting board with clean kitchen or paper towels and lay the zucchini sheets out in a single layer. Season lightly with salt and top with another layer of towels. Let rest for 15 minutes.

In a small bowl, beat the egg, then fold in the ricotta cheese. In a 9 × 12-inch ceramic baking dish, evenly distribute one-third of the roasted tomatoes over the bottom, then cover with a layer of zucchini sheets, then one-third of the ricotta mixture, and one-third of the spinach. Repeat this twice and top with a layer of zucchini.

Cover the dish with foil and bake for 30 minutes. Remove the foil, top with the mozzarella, and bake, uncovered, until the cheese is golden brown, another 15 to 20 minutes. Remove from the oven and let rest for 15 minutes, then slice and serve hot.

3 large tomatoes, cored and halved horizontally

Fine sea salt and freshly ground white pepper

1 tablespoon extra-virgin olive oil

1 teaspoon canola oil

1½ pounds spinach, rinsed and drained

1 garlic clove, coarsely chopped

3 large zucchini

1 egg

1 cup whole-milk ricotta cheese

½ cup shredded mozzarella cheese (2 ounces)

SPECIAL EQUIPMENT

Parchment paper

Vegetable sheet cutter or large mandoline

BLACK TRUFFLE TARTINE

SERVES 4

2 ounces Périgord black truffle, gently brushed clean

2 tablespoons unsalted butter, at room temperature

4 slices (¼ inch thick) Pullman or brioche loaf, crust removed

Scant 1 teaspoon canola oil

Fleur de sel

SPECIAL EQUIPMENT

Parchment paper

Truffle slicer/shaver or mandoline

Pastry brush

Black truffle season runs from December to March, and I anticipate it with excitement each year. As well as being very earthy, black truffles keep their flavor when cooked, unlike white truffles. In fact, slight heat actually *enhances* their flavor. Shaved onto a tartine is the simplest and best way to savor these black diamonds.

There are many species of truffle, and when you are shopping for black truffles it's essential to find those labeled *Tuber melanosporum*. As truffles are an expensive item, it's also important to know what traits to look for: A good truffle is firm and fragrant. To accurately define the complex aroma of truffles, I find it's helpful to use terms like a sommelier would with wine: They are earthy, mushroomy, with wet foliage and mineral characteristics. When you slice into the truffle, the inside is paler than the skin. A mature truffle's veins should be grayish and evenly spread throughout the flesh.

PREHEAT THE OVEN TO 250°F. Line a sheet pan with parchment paper.

Use a truffle slicer/shaver to very thinly slice the truffle. Arrange the slices on a single layer on the pan.

Using a pastry brush, spread a thin layer of softened butter on both sides of each slice of bread. Heat a large sauté pan over medium-low heat and toast the bread on both sides until golden brown.

Brush a small amount of oil onto each truffle slice and warm in the oven for 1 minute. Season the truffle slices with fleur de sel and divide them among the four slices of toast. Serve immediately.

SPICY SAUTÉED SHIITAKES

SERVES 4

The meatier the mushroom, the better. Thin shiitakes can get a bit soggy, but the meatier ones keep a better texture and get a nicer color. I make these at home often and they have quickly become one of my family's favorite snacks.

IN A LARGE SAUTÉ PAN, heat the oil over medium-high heat. When hot, add the mushrooms, season with a pinch of salt, and sauté until golden brown, about 2 minutes. Reduce the heat to medium, add the garlic, Sriracha, and herbes de Provence, and sauté, stirring regularly, until the mushrooms are tender, another 2 minutes. Taste and season with more salt and serve hot.

1 tablespoon canola oil

1 pound shiitake mushrooms, stems discarded, caps halved

Fine sea salt

1 garlic clove, thinly sliced

1 tablespoon Sriracha sauce

1 teaspoon herbes de Provence

BAKED CREMINI, "SNAIL BUTTER"

SERVES 4

6 tablespoons (¾ stick) unsalted butter, at room temperature

3 tablespoons finely chopped fresh parsley leaves

1 garlic clove, finely chopped

24 medium cremini mushrooms, stems removed

Fine sea salt and freshly ground white pepper

¼ cup fine dried bread crumbs

A play on the classic escargot, these make a fun and delicious canapé, or even a side dish for white meat. Button mushrooms work well here, too.

PREHEAT THE OVEN TO 425°F.

In a medium bowl, combine the butter, parsley, and garlic and mix well. Refrigerate until firm, about 20 minutes.

Place the mushrooms, stem sides up, in a baking dish or pie plate that's just large enough to hold them tightly packed. Season with salt and white pepper. Using a small spoon, fill each mushroom cavity with some of the butter mixture. Top each mushroom with bread crumbs.

Bake until the bread crumbs are golden brown, 12 to 14 minutes. Remove from the oven, arrange the mushrooms on a serving plate, and serve hot.

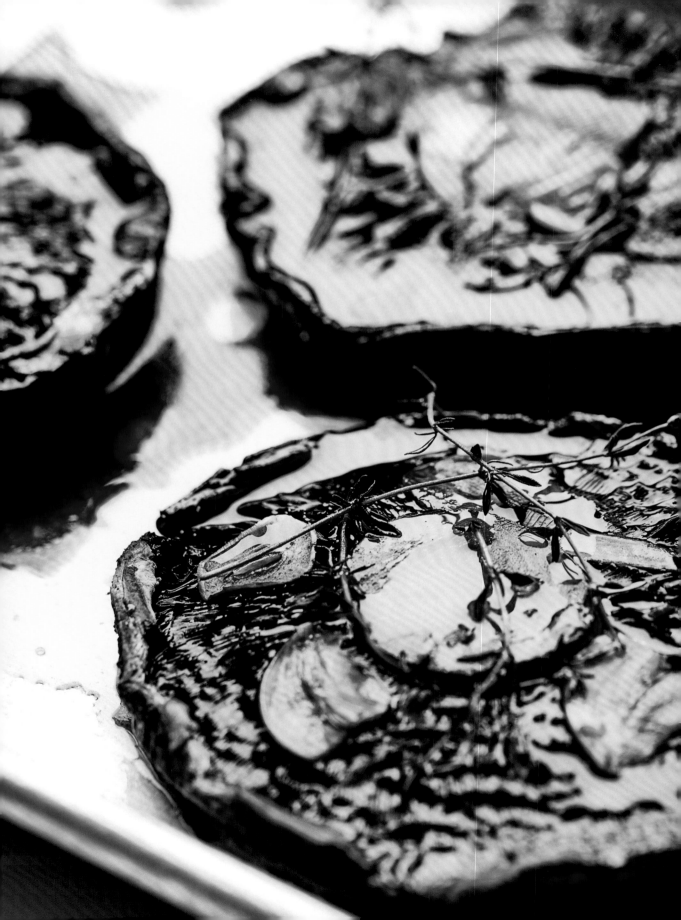

ROASTED PORTOBELLOS

SERVES 4

Portobello mushrooms are very meaty and can be eaten as a stand-alone dish, but you can also serve them as a side or garnish. It's important to wash the mushrooms thoroughly, and to keep the gills, as they have a lot of flavor. Save the cooking juices and pour them over the mushrooms just before serving, or allow your guests to do it themselves.

8 medium portobello mushrooms, cleaned and stems removed

Fine sea salt and freshly ground black pepper

2 garlic cloves, thinly sliced

8 to 16 sprigs thyme

4 tablespoons extra-virgin olive oil

PREHEAT THE OVEN TO 450°F.

In a baking dish, arrange the mushrooms, gill side up, in a single layer. Season the mushrooms with salt and pepper, then place 2 or 3 slices of garlic and 1 or 2 sprigs of thyme on each cap. Drizzle each mushroom with ½ tablespoon olive oil.

Transfer to the oven to roast until the flesh is very tender, 8 to 10 minutes.

Remove the mushrooms from the oven, arrange on a platter, and spoon the cooking juices over the top. Serve hot.

WHOLE ROASTED MAITAKE

SERVES 4

1 tablespoon grated fresh ginger (from a 1-inch piece)

¼ cup soy sauce

¼ cup rice vinegar

½ cup canola oil

4 whole maitake mushrooms (4 to 5 ounces each)

Fine sea salt and freshly ground white pepper

2 scallions, thinly sliced

Maitake, also known as hen of the woods, is a delicate mushroom in both texture and flavor, and cooking it whole preserves these qualities. They look great when served individually, and if you have a large one, it's fun to present it family style.

PREHEAT THE OVEN TO 400°F.

In a bowl, combine the ginger, soy sauce, and vinegar. Whisk in the oil. Set aside.

Arrange the mushrooms in a baking dish, add ¼ cup of water, and season the mushrooms with salt and white pepper.

Cover the dish with foil, transfer to the oven, and roast for 15 minutes. Remove the foil and roast until the mushrooms have taken on a little color, another 3 to 5 minutes.

Remove the mushrooms from the oven and carefully transfer them to four serving bowls. Gently dress the mushrooms with the vinaigrette, garnish with the scallions, and serve hot.

MORELS À LA CRÈME

SERVES 4

Every spring, I look forward to morel season. This classic dish pays homage to this magnificent mushroom. Dry sherry is essential here, as it helps draw out all the morel flavors.

FILL A BOWL with warm water and add the morels, gently washing to remove any dirt or debris. Drain and repeat the process until the water is clear. Pat the mushrooms dry.

In a large sauté pan, heat the oil over medium heat. Add the shallot, reduce the heat to medium-low, and sweat the shallot until just translucent, 3 to 4 minutes.

Add the morels and season with salt and white pepper. Increase the heat to medium-high and cook the mushrooms until they begin to soften, about 3 minutes. Add the cream and continue to cook until it is reduced by half, 3 to 5 minutes.

Add the sherry and cook for 1 minute. Taste the liquid and adjust the seasoning, as needed. Transfer to a serving dish, add the chives, and serve hot.

1½ pounds large morel mushrooms, stems trimmed

½ teaspoon canola oil

½ small shallot, finely diced

Fine sea salt and freshly ground white pepper

1 cup heavy cream

1 tablespoon dry sherry

2 teaspoons very thinly sliced chives

BLACK TRUFFLE QUESADILLAS

SERVES 4

1 cup masa harina
(nixtamalized corn flour)

Fine sea salt

1 tablespoon corn oil

½ cup Cotija cheese (about
2 ounces crumbled)

2 ounces Périgord black truffle,
thinly sliced on a mandoline or
truffle slicer/shaver, crumbs
reserved

2 tablespoons canola oil

2 teaspoons balsamic vinegar

2 tablespoons extra-virgin
olive oil

3 cups frisée lettuce, washed
and patted dry

SPECIAL EQUIPMENT

Truffle slicer/shaver or
mandoline

Stand mixer with dough hook
(optional)

Parchment paper

Tortilla press

I like the texture of these homemade tortillas, but you can save time by buying them. I prefer to use corn tortillas, as they have a touch of sweetness and more character than flour tortillas. The cheese enhances the flavor of the truffle, but this dish is really just another clever way to eat black truffles. I like to sip on some tequila reposado while I eat these. . . .

IN A BOWL, mix together the masa harina and a pinch of salt. In a separate bowl, combine the corn oil and ¾ cup of warm water. Slowly add half the water mixture to the corn flour, while stirring to form a sandy mix. Continue to stir, while slowly adding the remaining water mixture until the dough forms a slightly sticky ball. Knead this dough for 5 minutes by hand (or in a stand mixer fitted with the dough hook). You may need to add a bit more masa harina to keep the dough from getting too sticky.

Divide the dough into four portions and roll each into a ball.

Place a sheet of parchment paper on the surface of a tortilla press. Place a dough ball in the center of the press, top with another sheet of parchment, and close the tortilla press, pushing firmly to create a flat tortilla. Remove the tortilla from the press, peel off the parchment paper, and set the tortilla aside. Repeat with the remaining dough balls. (If you don't have a tortilla press, place the dough ball between parchment paper and press down firmly with a large pan until the dough spreads to a round tortilla about ⅛ inch thick.)

Heat a large nonstick sauté pan over medium-high heat. Add the tortillas one at a time and cook until they begin to get browned and slightly puffed up in spots, 1 to 2 minutes per side.

Set the tortillas on a sheet pan. Divide the Cotija cheese and shaved truffles evenly among the four tortillas, then fold each one in half, pressing down to seal them closed.

Place two large nonstick sauté pans over medium-high heat and add 1 tablespoon canola oil to each. Add two quesadillas to each pan and sauté until the tortillas are golden brown on both sides and the cheese is melted, about 2 minutes per side.

In a small bowl, combine the vinegar and a small pinch of salt. Whisk in the olive oil and any reserved truffle crumbs. In a medium bowl, dress the frisée with the vinaigrette.

Cut each quesadilla into four wedges. Divide them among four plates and serve with the frisée on the side.

TOMATO "CROQUE SEL"

SERVES 4

This is the easiest recipe in the book. The quality of the tomatoes makes this simple "dish" incredible. The tomatoes have to be spectacular, so it is well worth your time to seek out the best ones you can find (see my tips on how to shop for produce on page 231). While it's such a light snack, it's still utterly satisfying—the ultimate simple pleasure.

4 large ripe-to-perfection tomatoes, cored and halved horizontally through the equator

Freshly ground black pepper

Extra-virgin olive oil

Fleur de sel or coarse salt

SEASON EACH TOMATO with pepper and extra-virgin olive oil. Finish with fleur de sel and serve.

BREAKFAST RADISH, BUTTER, SALT

SERVES 4

24 breakfast or globe radishes

6 tablespoons (¾ stick) unsalted butter, at room temperature

1 tablespoon kosher salt or fine sea salt

I find radishes are best in spring when they are small and their peppery flavor is subtle, but you can use larger ones with a more intense flavor here if that's to your taste. The French use creamy butter to contrast with the crisp texture, and salt to balance the sweet and spicy essence. Submerging the radishes in ice water makes them extra crisp and helps them open like a flower once they've been scored.

SET UP A BOWL of ice and water. If the radish greens are in good shape, leave them intact. If not, trim and discard the greens. Use a sharp paring knife to score an X into the top one-third to one-half of each radish. Place the radishes in the ice and let sit for 3 minutes, so the X opens up and the radishes become crisp. Remove and pat dry.

To serve, spread butter into the center of the opening in each radish top using a butter knife, then sprinkle with salt and enjoy.

HEARTS OF PALM, MUSTARD VINAIGRETTE

SERVES 4

I love canned hearts of palm, as their quality is very consistent. I often eat them straight out of the can, dipping them in the sauce. The sharp mustard complements their smooth flavor perfectly.

IN A BOWL, combine the vinegars and season with a pinch of salt. Add the mustard and whisk until well combined. Slowly whisk in the oil to emulsify. Stir in the shallot and chives and season with salt and white pepper.

Season the hearts of palm with salt and white pepper. Gently toss with the vinaigrette and serve on a platter.

2 tablespoons sherry vinegar

2 tablespoons red wine vinegar

Fine sea salt

2 tablespoons Dijon mustard

½ cup canola oil

1 teaspoon finely chopped shallot

1 teaspoon finely sliced chives

Freshly ground white pepper

1 pound fresh or canned hearts of palm, cut into sections

SUMMER ROLL

SERVES 4

4 rice paper rounds
(about 8 inches)

1 cup mesclun greens

20 fresh mint leaves

20 fresh basil leaves

20 fresh cilantro leaves

½ red bell pepper, cut into
3-inch-long julienne

½ yellow bell pepper, cut into
3-inch-long julienne

1 Persian (mini) cucumber,
cut into 3-inch-long julienne

¼ large carrot, cut into
3-inch-long julienne

1 avocado, cut into
¼-inch-thick wedges, rubbed
with lime juice

Fine sea salt and freshly
ground white pepper

Light, bright, and refreshing in the warmer months, these rolls are healthy and delicious—which is good because you'll definitely reach for more than one. Rice paper is common in Vietnamese cuisine and can be found in most grocery stores.

HALF-FILL A LARGE BOWL with warm water. Line a large plate with damp paper towels.

Submerge a rice paper round in the warm water, letting it soak for about 30 seconds, until pliable. Remove it from the water and lay it flat on a clean, dry cutting board.

In the center of the rice paper, leaving a 2-inch margin on the top and bottom, create a single layer of mesclun mix, then a layer of herbs (3 to 5 leaves of each variety), followed by a single layer each of red and yellow pepper, cucumber, and carrot, and a row of avocado slices. Season with salt and white pepper.

Pull the bottom end of the paper up to cover the vegetable filling about one-third of the way. Pull one side of the paper over the vegetables to cover them completely, and tuck and roll the other sides tightly to complete the log. The paper will adhere to itself. Set the roll on the plate with the damp paper towels and loosely cover.

Repeat the procedure with the remaining rice paper rounds and vegetable filling.

When ready to serve, cut each roll into 6 to 8 pieces and serve immediately.

BLISTERED SHISHITO PEPPERS

SERVES 4

One in ten of these peppers is ultraspicy, but the other nine are sweet—so good luck! When you fry them you need to make sure they are fully blistered, but be careful because if they burst, they release liquid into the hot oil and it can splatter.

Canola oil

6 ounces shishito peppers (about 40 pieces)

Fine sea salt

LINE A SHEET PAN or a large plate with paper towels. In a large sauté pan, heat ¼ inch of canola oil over medium-high heat.

Carefully add the peppers to the pan and cook, turning each pepper once or twice with tongs, until they are blistered on all sides, 1 to 2 minutes per side. Transfer the peppers to the paper towels to drain. Season with salt and serve hot.

WHOLE ROASTED GARLIC

SERVES 4

2 heads garlic, halved
horizontally through the
equator

Fine sea salt and freshly
ground white pepper

2 tablespoons extra-virgin
olive oil

16 slices (¼ inch thick)
baguette

Roasting whole garlic brings out its sweetness and makes the sharp, raw garlic flavor disappear. Spread the cloves directly on a sliced baguette or store them in a tightly sealed container in the fridge to add to sauce or dressings.

PREHEAT THE OVEN TO 400°F.

In a small baking pan, arrange the garlic heads with cut sides facing up and add 1 tablespoon of water. Season the garlic with salt and white pepper and drizzle the olive oil over each head. Cover the pan tightly with foil.

Roast in the oven for 40 minutes. Remove the foil and roast another 15 minutes, until the garlic is browned and easily pierced with a paring knife (it should be soft and spreadable). Remove from the oven.

Arrange the baguette slices on a baking sheet and toast in the oven, 3 to 4 minutes. Arrange them on a platter and serve with the hot garlic.

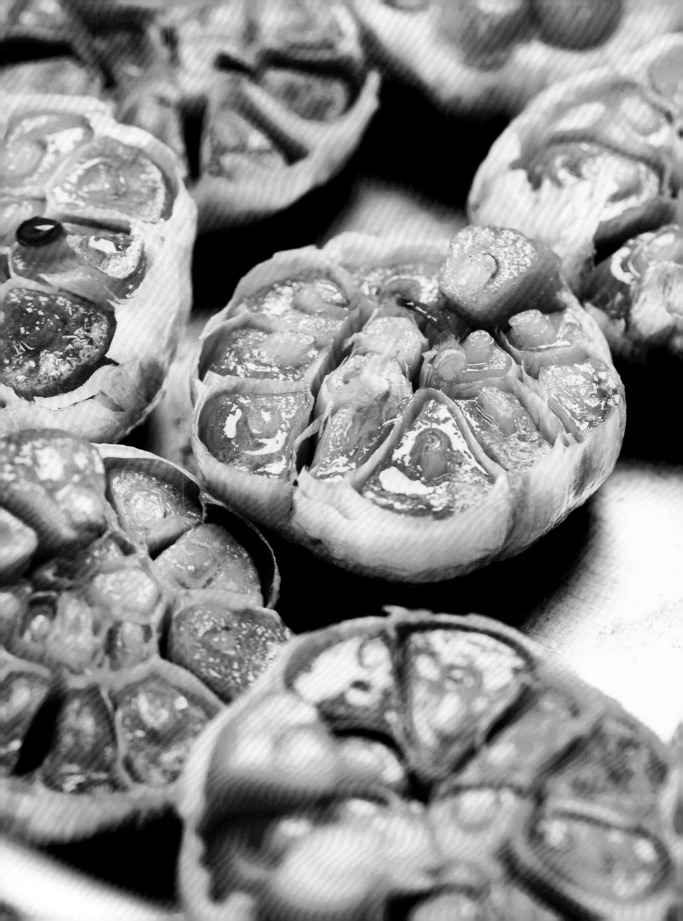

BABY STRING BEANS AU BEURRE

SERVES 4

In early spring, young green beans are so tender, and while they have a natural rich, buttery flavor, we still add more butter. When seasoned with some salt and pepper, absolutely nothing else is needed.

Fine sea salt

1 pound haricots verts or very thin green beans, ends trimmed

Freshly ground white pepper

2 tablespoons unsalted butter

IN A MEDIUM POT, bring 4 quarts of water to a boil and season with salt. Add the beans and cook until tender but still bright green, about 5 minutes.

Drain the beans and transfer them to a platter. Season with salt and white pepper, distribute the butter over the hot beans, and serve immediately.

YUKON GOLD POTATOES, BUTTER, CHIVES

SERVES 4

2 pounds small Yukon Gold potatoes

Fine sea salt

4 tablespoons (½ stick) unsalted butter, diced

2 tablespoons finely sliced chives

Freshly ground white pepper

There are endless ways to prepare potatoes and this is one of the simplest and tastiest. If I'm making a potato salad, I combine them with mustard and mayonnaise instead of butter. Never refrigerate raw potatoes, as the cold kills their flavor.

IN A LARGE POT, combine the potatoes with water to cover by 1 inch and season with fine sea salt. Bring to a boil and cook until potatoes are tender, 12 to 14 minutes. Drain, reserving 2 tablespoons of potato cooking liquid.

When the potatoes are cool enough to handle, peel with a paring knife and keep them warm in a covered bowl.

In a small saucepan, bring the reserved cooking liquid to a simmer and whisk in the butter a few pieces at a time, until it has all been incorporated.

Add the butter emulsion to the potatoes and gently toss to coat. Add the chives, season with salt and white pepper, and serve hot.

GRILLED CORN ELOTE STYLE

SERVES 4

When corn is at its sweetest, I love to grill it until it caramelizes on the outside. On its own, it's delicious, but this corn preparation is next level. Buy more ears of corn than you think you'll need, as I guarantee you will want more.

IN A SMALL BOWL, whisk together the mayonnaise and lime juice. Season to taste with the salt and set aside.

Heat a grill to medium-high. Grill the ears of corn, turning them occasionally, until the kernels are cooked through and lightly charred, 8 to 10 minutes total.

Let the corn cool for a few minutes. Scatter the Cotija cheese and cilantro on a flat plate. Using a pastry brush, lightly coat each ear with the mayonnaise mixture and then roll each ear in the cheese/cilantro mixture. Season each with a pinch of cayenne, and serve with lime wedges alongside.

¼ cup mayonnaise

Juice of 1 lime, plus 1 lime quartered

Fine sea salt

4 ears corn, shucked

½ cup Cotija cheese, crumbled

¼ cup fresh cilantro leaves, coarsely chopped

Cayenne pepper or red pepper flakes

SPECIAL EQUIPMENT

Grill

Pastry brush

GRILLED EGGPLANT, MISO

SERVES 4

¼ cup red miso

2 tablespoons mirin

1 tablespoon sake

4 Japanese eggplants, sliced into 36 coins (½ inch thick)

1 teaspoon canola oil

1 tablespoon toasted sesame seeds (optional)

SPECIAL EQUIPMENT

24 bamboo skewers

Grill or grill pan

Pastry brush

Japanese eggplant is best to use here, as it's the perfect size and not too seedy. Its flesh is sweeter and more tender than regular eggplant, and it is the perfect, smoky vehicle for the salty, umami miso.

SOAK THE BAMBOO SKEWERS in water for at least 10 minutes.

In a small bowl, stir together the miso, mirin, and sake.

Use two skewers for 3 eggplant coins. Slide the eggplant onto the skewers, arranging the skewers parallel to one another and close to the edges of each eggplant coin. Repeat with the remaining pairs of skewers and eggplant coins for a total of 12.

Heat a grill or grill pan to medium-high and oil lightly. Grill the eggplant for 2 minutes, then flip, brush with the miso mixture, and grill 2 more minutes.

Garnish with sesame seeds (if using) and serve hot.

SAUTÉED SWEET PLANTAINS

SERVES 4

My dear friend, chef Alfredo Ayala, taught me how to make these many years ago in Puerto Rico. The savory rosemary is a surprising complement to the sweet plantains.

2 tablespoons unsalted butter

16 ripe yellow baby plantains, peeled

4 large sprigs rosemary

Fine sea salt

LINE A PLATE with paper towels. Heat a large sauté pan over medium heat and add the butter. Once the butter has foamed and the bubbles have subsided, add the plantains and sauté until they're beginning to brown, about 3 minutes. Add the rosemary and continue to sauté until the plantains are golden brown, 2 to 3 minutes. Remove the plantains from the pan and let drain on the paper towels. Season with salt and serve hot.

SAUTÉED PEA SHOOTS
HONG KONG STYLE

SERVES 4

1 tablespoon grated
peeled fresh ginger
(about a 1-inch piece)

1 small garlic clove,
finely chopped

2 tablespoons fresh lime juice

2 tablespoons soy sauce

¼ cup plus 1 tablespoon
canola oil

½ cup fresh sweet peas

8 cups pea shoots
(about ½ pound)

Fine sea salt and freshly
ground white pepper

Pea shoots are at their most tender and sweet in early spring. The cooking process is very fast and the key is to achieve the texture combination of crunchy stems and soft, slightly wilted leaves. I cook this in a wok but a sauté pan will do.

IN A SMALL BOWL, combine the ginger, garlic, lime juice, soy sauce, and ¼ cup of the canola oil. Mix the vinaigrette well and set aside.

Set up a large bowl of ice and water. Bring a medium pot of salted water to a boil, blanch peas for 1 minute. Drain and shock in the ice water until cool, then set aside.

In a large wok or sauté pan, heat the remaining 1 tablespoon canola oil over high heat. Add the pea shoots and peas and cook until the greens are just wilted, about 1 minute. Add 1 tablespoon of the vinaigrette and toss to coat. Season the vegetables with salt and white pepper to taste, then remove from the heat.

To serve, divide the pea shoots and peas among four plates, drizzle some of the remaining vinaigrette over each, and serve hot.

BOK CHOY, SOY-GINGER VINAIGRETTE

SERVES 4

When you cook bok choy, its heart should stay firm while the leaves become soft and tender. Take care to not over- or undercook it by monitoring its doneness. If you place a paring knife through the heart of the bok choy, you should be able to pull it out with no resistance. To keep the leaves together, cook the bok choy whole and then split it in half before serving.

IN A SMALL BOWL, combine the shallot, ginger, soy sauce, and lime juice. Slowly whisk in the oil and set aside.

In a large pot, bring 4 quarts of water to a boil and season with a large pinch of salt. Add the bok choy and cook until tender, about 5 minutes.

Drain the bok choy, halve lengthwise, and season lightly with salt and white pepper. Divide among four plates and drizzle the vinaigrette over each one. Serve hot or at room temperature.

½ tablespoon finely chopped shallot

½ tablespoon grated fresh ginger

2 tablespoons soy sauce

2 tablespoons fresh lime juice

¼ cup canola oil

Fine sea salt

16 large heads bok choy, trimmed and rinsed

Freshly ground white pepper

SAUTÉED BROCCOLINI

SERVES 4

2 tablespoons extra-virgin olive oil

2 bunches broccolini, florets separated and stem ends discarded

2 garlic cloves, thinly sliced

Fine sea salt

1 teaspoon red pepper flakes

Juice of ½ lemon

Broccolini is a cross between broccoli and its leafy cousin, Chinese broccoli. It has longer stalks and smaller, looser florets. It's a little bitter, a little sweet, and a great, quick option for a side dish. I like to keep it simple.

HEAT A LARGE SAUTÉ PAN over medium-high heat and add the olive oil. Add the broccolini and the garlic, reduce the heat to medium, and season with salt. Sauté over medium heat until the garlic is golden and the broccolini is tender, 6 to 8 minutes.

Add the pepper flakes and lemon juice and serve hot.

BAKED SWEET POTATO

SERVES 4

This dish uses the same process as a regular baked potato, but it feels a bit more unusual with its orange color and sweet taste. If you are lucky enough to have a real fireplace or a fire pit, you can wrap the potatoes in foil and place them on the ashes for a pleasant, smoky flavor.

4 large sweet potatoes

1 teaspoon canola oil, plus more, as needed

Fine sea salt and freshly ground white pepper

6 tablespoons crème fraîche

1 tablespoon finely sliced chives

PREHEAT THE OVEN TO 425°F.

Gently pierce the sweet potatoes with a skewer or a paring knife and rub the skin with the canola oil. Season with salt and white pepper and bake on a sheet pan until tender, about 1 hour.

Let the potatoes rest for 10 minutes, then slice them open lengthwise, season with salt and white pepper, and top each potato with 1½ tablespoons of crème fraîche. Garnish with chives and serve hot.

WARM GOLDEN BEETS, AGED BALSAMIC

SERVES 4

8 medium golden or yellow beets, greens trimmed off

1 cup red wine vinegar

Fine sea salt

½ cup aged balsamic vinegar

Freshly ground white pepper

I love beets in general for their earthy and sweet flavor. Red beets can be challenging because they stain everything they touch; golden beets, on the other hand, are similar in taste but don't stain. It's imperative to put red wine vinegar in the water when cooking, as it brings some sourness to cut the excess sweetness of the beets.

IN A MEDIUM-LARGE POT, combine the beets with water to cover by 3 inches. Add the red wine vinegar and a large pinch of salt and bring to a simmer. Cook at a simmer until the beets are tender, 60 to 75 minutes, adding water as necessary to keep them submerged. Using a paring knife, pierce the top of a beet to check if tender. The tip of the knife should easily penetrate the beet.

Meanwhile, in a small saucepan, bring the balsamic vinegar to a simmer and cook until reduced by half, 8 to 12 minutes. Transfer the reduced balsamic to a container to cool.

Remove the beets from the heat and let them cool in the cooking liquid. When they are cool enough to handle, slip off the skins and discard them, and slice each beet in half. Season with salt and white pepper, drizzle with the reduced balsamic, and serve.

GREEN ASPARAGUS TEMPURA

SERVES 4

You need thick asparagus for this, and the tempura is not difficult once you learn the technique. The goal is to get the coating crisp and the asparagus al dente. A little trick the chef Jean-Louis Palladin, my mentor, shared with me: If you don't have tempura or cake flour, add a tiny pinch of baking soda to all-purpose flour for a super light, crispy batter.

IN A DEEP POT, pour 4 inches of rice bran oil or canola oil and the sesame oil. Heat over medium-high heat to 350°F on a deep-fry thermometer.

In a bowl, combine 1 cup of the flour and the sparkling water and gently mix, leaving the batter slightly lumpy. Stir in the egg.

Dust the asparagus with the remaining ¼ cup flour, patting off the excess, then transfer to the batter.

Line a sheet pan or large plate with paper towels. Working in batches (to avoid overcrowding), use chopsticks or tongs to gently transfer the asparagus to the hot oil. Cook until the asparagus spears have floated to the surface and are no longer bubbling, about 2 minutes. They should be pale in color and very crisp. Remove the cooked asparagus to the paper towels to drain. Season with salt.

In a small bowl, whisk together the soy sauce, mirin, and lime juice. Divide this mixture among four small bowls and serve alongside the asparagus.

Rice bran oil or canola oil for frying

2 tablespoons sesame oil

1¼ cups Japanese tempura flour or cake flour

1 cup ice-cold sparkling water

1 large egg, beaten

20 asparagus spears (about 6 inches long), peeled from the tip down

Fine sea salt

3 tablespoons soy sauce

1 tablespoon mirin

1 tablespoon fresh lime juice

SPECIAL EQUIPMENT

Deep-fry/candy thermometer

Chopsticks or tongs

POACHED GREEN ASPARAGUS, HOLLANDAISE SAUCE

SERVES 4

Fine sea salt

2½ sticks (10 ounces) unsalted butter

20 thick green asparagus spears (about 6 inches long), peeled from the tip down

2 egg yolks

1 tablespoon Dijon mustard

2 tablespoons fresh lemon juice

Freshly ground white pepper

SPECIAL EQUIPMENT

Kitchen twine

Blender

One of my favorite ways to eat green asparagus, this dish contrasts the richness of the hollandaise with the grassy asparagus. Hollandaise purists will disagree, but there's no need for clarified butter here, as we use a blender, and the sauce will hold without it.

IN A LARGE POT, bring 6 cups of water to a boil and add 1 teaspoon salt. In a separate small pot, melt the butter and bring to a simmer, then remove from the direct heat source, but keep hot.

Cut four 12-inch lengths of kitchen twine. Make two bundles of 10 asparagus spears each and tie them with the kitchen twine 2 inches from the top and 2 inches from the bottom. Add the asparagus to the boiling water and cook until just tender, 5 to 7 minutes.

While the asparagus cooks, in a blender, combine the yolks, mustard, and lemon juice and blend at medium speed, slowly drizzling in the hot melted butter in a steady stream. Once the butter has been fully incorporated, season the mixture with salt and white pepper and transfer to a serving pot, keeping it warm.

Divide the asparagus among four plates and serve with the hollandaise sauce poured over the top.

FERRAN ADRIÀ POTATO FOAM

SERVES 4

There are many delicious forms of mashed potato, and one of the most famous (perhaps *the* most famous) is a recipe created by my mentor Joël Robuchon. However, Ferran Adrià invented something truly magical by breaking the mold entirely and making this cloud-like potato. Serve the foam immediately to maintain the ultralight texture.

½ pound Yukon Gold potatoes (1 to 2 medium)

Fine sea salt

¾ cup milk

4 tablespoons (½ stick) unsalted butter

Freshly ground white pepper

IN A LARGE POT, combine the potatoes with water to cover by 2 inches and season with 1 teaspoon salt. Bring the water to a simmer and cook the potatoes until tender and easily pierced with a paring knife, about 30 minutes. Drain the potatoes and let them cool for a few minutes.

Use a paring knife to gently peel the hot potatoes.

In a small saucepot, heat the milk over low heat until warm.

Place the potatoes in a ricer or food mill and process them into a medium saucepan. Add the butter, reduce the heat to low, and gently whisk in the warmed milk. Do not overmix, to keep the potatoes from becoming tacky. The mixture should be the consistency of a thick milkshake. Taste the mixture and season with salt and white pepper.

Transfer half the mixture to an iSi canister, seal it, and charge the contents of the canister twice with whipped cream chargers. Dispense the potato foam into two serving bowls. Once you have emptied the canister, repeat with the remaining potato mixture. Serve hot.

SPECIAL EQUIPMENT

Ricer/food mill

iSi whipper (with whipped cream chargers)

VEGETABLE SIMPLE

POACHED DAIKON, KIMCHI BROTH

SERVES 4

1 large daikon radish, peeled, halved lengthwise, and cut into 16 half-moons (½ inch thick)

Fine sea salt

1 cup kimchi, with juice

½ cup rice vinegar

3 tablespoons mirin

1 tablespoon soy sauce

Daikon radishes have a very light texture and a very distinctive, powerful, turnip-like taste. On a cold day they are delicious with kimchi broth. The spiciness warms you immediately.

IN A SAUCEPAN, combine the daikon slices with 2 quarts of water. Season with 1 teaspoon salt, bring to a simmer, and cook until tender, 10 to 12 minutes. Scoop out 1 cup of the poaching broth.

In a separate saucepan, combine the cup of daikon poaching broth, kimchi and its juice, vinegar, mirin, and soy sauce. Bring to a simmer and cook for 10 minutes. Transfer the mixture to a blender and puree. Then strain it into a clean pot and keep warm, discarding the solids.

Drain the daikon and distribute among four warmed bowls. Ladle the kimchi broth into each bowl and serve hot.

SPECIAL EQUIPMENT

Blender

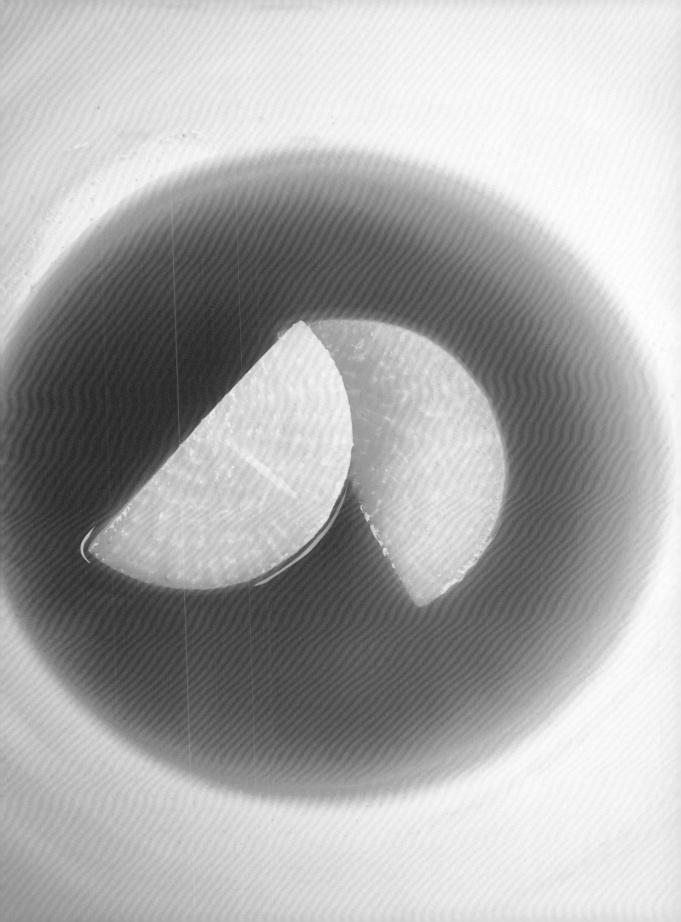

VEGETABLE PISTOU

SERVES 4

My aunt Monique would make this every year in the middle of August. While it's a simple dish, it's a true homage to vegetables and became such an occasion in my family that my cousins and I would get excited when my aunt would start making it. Our whole family would gather at long tables in the garden on those warm August evenings in Provence to eat this pistou together. Don't be intimated by the number of ingredients. The recipe is lengthy, but the bulk of the work is prepping and cutting the vegetables, which you can start a day in advance.

PLACE THE BEANS IN A BOWL, add water to cover by 1 inch, and refrigerate overnight.

Drain the beans and transfer them to a medium pot. Add 3 cups of water and bring to a simmer. Cook at a simmer until the beans are very tender, about 1 hour. Once the beans are almost cooked, season them with salt and white pepper, then stir in the onion, carrot, zucchini, green beans, and tomato and cook for 10 to 12 minutes.

Meanwhile, bring a pot of lightly salted water to a boil. Set up a bowl of ice and water nearby. Blanch the basil in the boiling water for 30 seconds, then drain and quickly transfer to the ice bath. When cool, gently squeeze out the excess water and transfer to a blender. Add the garlic and with the blender on low speed, slowly stream in the oil. Puree the pesto and season with salt and white pepper.

Stir the pesto into the beans and vegetables, then taste and adjust the seasoning if necessary. Divide the pistou among four warmed bowls and serve hot.

½ cup dried small white beans (navy beans)

Fine sea salt and freshly ground white pepper

¼ small onion, cut into ¼-inch dice

1 medium carrot, cut into ¼-inch dice

½ medium zucchini, cut into ¼-inch dice

12 to 15 green beans, ends trimmed, cut into ¼-inch dice

1 medium tomato, peeled, seeded, and cut into ¼-inch dice

3 cups loosely packed fresh basil leaves (about 1 large bunch)

1 garlic clove, coarsely chopped

⅓ cup extra-virgin olive oil

SPECIAL EQUIPMENT

Blender

STUFFED ZUCCHINI FLOWERS

SERVES 4

½ teaspoon canola oil

¾ cup finely diced zucchini

Fine sea salt

1 cup ricotta cheese

2 teaspoons finely chopped fresh mint leaves

Finely grated zest of 1 small lemon (about a scant teaspoon)

Freshly ground white pepper

16 large zucchini flowers, stamens removed

1 teaspoon salted butter

SPECIAL EQUIPMENT

Pastry bag (or zip-top plastic bag with one corner cut out)

Zucchini flowers are delicate, with a unique flavor. They are also aesthetically beautiful, so they make an impressive summer canapé or garnish. Make sure they are fully cooked, as they can be difficult and messy to cut into if they are underdone.

IN A SAUTÉ PAN, warm the canola oil over medium heat. Add the zucchini and a pinch of salt and cook until soft, about 3 minutes. Remove it from the pan and set aside to cool.

Preheat the oven to 350°F.

Place the ricotta cheese in a bowl. Once the zucchini is cool, fold it into the ricotta along with the mint, lemon zest, and salt and white pepper to taste.

Transfer the mixture to a pastry bag. Pipe the mixture into each flower and place them side by side in a baking pan. Add 2 tablespoons of water to cover the bottom of the pan and dot the butter around.

Bake until the filling is hot but the flowers have kept their shape, 5 to 7 minutes. Serve hot.

VEGETABLE POT-AU-FEU

SERVES 4

A warm and welcome appetizer on a cold day. The mushroom consommé can be prepared in advance (you can even freeze it if you are really planning ahead). The combination of the brown lentils and bay leaf brings another layer of meaty flavor, much like a "real" pot-au-feu.

TIE THE LENTILS AND BAY LEAF TOGETHER in a cheesecloth pouch. In a large pot, combine the pouch, 6 cups of water, the mushroom consommé, ginger, and garlic. Bring to a simmer and cook for 20 minutes.

Add the carrots, leeks, potatoes, mushrooms, and fennel and simmer for another 10 minutes. Add the cabbage and simmer another 10 minutes. Remove the pouch of lentils and bay leaf. Taste the broth and season with salt and white pepper, as needed.

Divide the vegetables and broth among four bowls and serve hot.

½ cup brown lentils

1 bay leaf

2 cups Mushroom Consommé (page 30)

1-inch piece fresh ginger, peeled and sliced

2 garlic cloves, peeled

8 baby carrots, peeled

8 baby leeks, green tops trimmed, roots removed

12 baby potatoes

12 button mushrooms, quartered

1 medium bulb fennel, cut through the core into 8 wedges with core intact

½ head napa cabbage, cut lengthwise through the core into 4 wedges with core intact

Fine sea salt and freshly ground white pepper

SPECIAL EQUIPMENT

Cheesecloth

VIETNAMESE PHO

SERVES 4

BROTH

3 shallots, coarsely chopped

8 garlic cloves, smashed

1 pound button mushrooms, coarsely chopped

3-inch piece fresh ginger, peeled and sliced

3 small radishes, coarsely chopped

1 small carrot, coarsely chopped

1 rib celery, coarsely chopped

½ stalk fresh lemongrass, coarsely chopped

2 teaspoons black peppercorns

2 pods star anise

1 whole clove

8 basil stems

8 cilantro stems

¼ cup soy sauce

Fine sea salt

GARNISH

8 ounces rice noodles

4 large shiitake mushrooms, stems discarded

Fine sea salt

1 cup soybean sprouts

2 scallions, thinly sliced

2 radishes, thinly sliced

2 tablespoons chiffonade-cut cilantro leaves

2 tablespoons chiffonade-cut basil leaves

1 lime, cut into wedges

This vegan pho is chock-full of flavor and textures. The meatiness of the shiitakes makes this light dish mighty and filling, and perfect for a winter evening.

MAKE THE BROTH: In a large pot, combine the shallots, garlic, mushrooms, ginger, radishes, carrot, celery, lemongrass, peppercorns, star anise, clove, and basil and cilantro stems. Add 8 cups of water and bring to a boil. Reduce the heat to a simmer and let cook for 1 hour, then add the soy sauce and season the mixture with salt. Strain and discard the solids, then return the broth to a saucepan and reduce to 6 cups.

Meanwhile, prepare the garnish: Fill a large saucepan with 3 quarts of water and bring to a boil. Add the rice noodles and cook until just barely tender, 3 to 4 minutes. Drain the noodles and rinse under cold water until cool. Set aside.

Bring the broth back to a high simmer. Season the shiitakes with salt and poach them in the broth for 3 to 4 minutes or just tender. Remove the shiitakes and slice each cap into 4 or 5 pieces.

Divide the cooked rice noodles among four warmed bowls and pour the hot broth over. Garnish each serving with sliced shiitakes, sprouts, scallions, radishes, cilantro, and basil and serve hot, with lime wedges alongside.

SLOW-ROASTED CAULIFLOWER

SERVES 4

This cauliflower is great to serve family style so your guests can share. I use shichimi togarashi here, but you can use any spices or herbs you wish, such as za'atar, herbes de Provence, or paprika.

PREHEAT THE OVEN TO 450°F. Place a wire rack on a sheet pan.

Fill a large pot with enough water to cover the cauliflower by 1 inch. Bring the water to a simmer and stir in 2 tablespoons of the togarashi and salt to taste. Add the cauliflower to the water, return to a simmer, and cook until you can insert a skewer, or the tip of a paring knife, into the core with some ease, 8 to 10 minutes. Remove the cauliflower from the pot and place it on the rack on the sheet pan.

Brush the cauliflower with the oil and transfer it to the oven to roast until it is very tender, but not yet falling apart, 15 to 20 minutes. To make sure it's not undercooked, test its doneness with a skewer or paring knife down through the center—it should come away easily. If the cauliflower starts to get too browned, you can cover it with foil until it is done cooking.

Remove it from the oven and sprinkle with the remaining 2 tablespoons togarashi and white pepper. Cut the head into 4 wedges and serve hot.

1 head cauliflower, including leaves

4 tablespoons shichimi togarashi

Fine sea salt

1 tablespoon canola oil

Freshly ground white pepper

SPECIAL EQUIPMENT

Wire rack

Pastry brush

GRANDMA'S BYALDI

SERVES 4

½ cup extra-virgin olive oil

4 medium yellow onions, quartered through the root and thinly sliced crosswise

Fine sea salt and freshly ground black pepper

4 Roma (plum) tomatoes, cored and cut into ⅛-inch-thick slices

1 medium zucchini, cut into ⅛-inch-thick slices

1 medium yellow summer squash, cut into ⅛-inch-thick slices

1 large Japanese eggplant, cut into ⅛-inch-thick slices

1 tablespoon fresh thyme leaves

Byaldi is a very typical Provençal dish similar to a very fancy ratatouille. My grandmother made it on Sundays to bring with us when we visited our extended family in the countryside. We would have to drive for hours, but we didn't mind because the smell of the byaldi in the car was so good. It took everything we had not to steal a piece before we arrived at my aunt Monique's house. We wouldn't even reheat it, we would just eat it warm from the casserole. It's even better the next day if you manage to have leftovers.

PREHEAT THE OVEN TO 450°F.

In a large pot, combine ¼ cup of the olive oil and the onions and cook over medium heat, stirring every few minutes, until they begin to brown and caramelize, 20 to 25 minutes.

Season the onions with salt and pepper and transfer them to a 10-inch casserole or baking dish, distributing them in an even layer over the bottom of the casserole.

Arrange a tight overlapping row of tomatoes along the edge of the casserole (as in the photo), then follow suit with the zucchini, summer squash, and eggplant, and another row of tomatoes, zucchini, squash, and eggplant, until you have filled the casserole with fanned rows of vegetables. Drizzle with the remaining ¼ cup olive oil, and season with the thyme and salt and pepper to taste.

Transfer to the oven and bake until the vegetables are tender and the casserole is bubbling and caramelized at the edges, 20 to 30 minutes.

Remove from the oven and let rest for 20 minutes in a warm place. Serve hot.

HERBES DE PROVENCE–CRUSTED TOMATOES

SERVES 4

This dish is inspired by tomatoes Provençal, but much simpler. Getting the right crust really makes these tomatoes stand out. Not only will the toasted herbs bring flavor, but they will also add a crunchiness to the texture. I like the tomatoes to be fully cooked with a jammy consistency here.

8 very ripe medium tomatoes, cored and halved horizontally through the equator

Fine sea salt and freshly ground black pepper

4 tablespoons herbes de Provence

4 tablespoons extra-virgin olive oil

ARRANGE THE TOMATOES, cut side up, on a plate and season each one with salt and pepper. Divide the herbes de Provence evenly among the tomatoes, firmly pressing the herbs to adhere them.

Heat a large sauté pan over medium-high heat and add 2 tablespoons of the olive oil. Carefully add the tomatoes to the pan, herbed side down, and cook for 2 to 3 minutes. Carefully flip the tomatoes and cook until soft and fully cooked, 2 to 3 minutes longer.

Transfer to a plate, drizzle with the remaining 2 tablespoons olive oil, and serve.

ROASTED DELICATA SQUASH

SERVES 4

½ cup plus 1 teaspoon canola oil

2 delicata squash, 1 halved lengthwise and seeded, 1 cut crosswise into four 2-inch-thick rounds and seeded

Fine sea salt and freshly ground white pepper

4 tablespoons (½ stick) unsalted butter, at room temperature

8 slices (¼ inch thick) baguette

4 large fresh sage leaves

SPECIAL EQUIPMENT

Pastry brush

Deep-fry/candy thermometer

Blender

I make this in the fall when the delicata are nicely ripe, otherwise they can be too starchy. Unlike most other squash, delicata squash skins can be eaten once they're cooked. Sage is the perfect herb to pair with the squash, and the croutons add a nice crunch.

PREHEAT THE OVEN TO 400°.

Oil a sheet pan with 1 teaspoon of the oil and arrange the squash halves and rounds on the pan. Season the squash with salt and white pepper. Using a pastry brush, coat the squash rounds with 2 tablespoons of the softened butter.

Roast in the oven until tender, 35 to 40 minutes. Remove the squash and let cool for 10 minutes.

Meanwhile, line a plate with paper towels. In a small pot, heat the remaining ½ cup canola oil to 350°F on a deep-fry thermometer. Fry the sage leaves, a few at a time, in the hot oil for 1 to 2 minutes and drain on the paper towels.

Use a spoon to scoop out the flesh of the squash halves and transfer to a blender. Add the remaining 2 tablespoons butter and puree until smooth, adding a splash of water to get the process started. Taste the puree and season with salt and white pepper to taste.

Return the squash rounds to the oven to warm through and, at the same time, toast the baguettes in the oven until golden brown, a few minutes.

Divide the squash rounds among four warmed plates. Fill the center of each round with squash puree. Garnish each plate with 2 baguette toasts and a sage leaf and serve.

BAKED BUTTERNUT SQUASH

SERVES 4

I like to roll my spoon through the soft baked squash, just like eating ice cream out of the container. Half a squash seems like a lot for one person but it's so light, you won't feel over-fed. I eat it as is and tend not to disrupt the pure flavor with any additional spices or seasoning.

2 medium butternut squash, halved lengthwise and seeded

2 tablespoons unsalted butter, diced

Fine sea salt and freshly ground white pepper

PREHEAT THE OVEN TO 350°F.

In a large baking dish, add water to barely cover the bottom of the pan, then add the squash, cut side down, and butter. Cover tightly with foil and bake until the squash is very tender and easily pierced with a paring knife, 50 to 60 minutes.

Remove from the oven, season with salt and white pepper, and serve.

ROASTED CARROTS, HARISSA

SERVES 4

1 tablespoon canola oil

4 small garlic cloves, thinly sliced

½ cup thinly sliced shallot (1 medium)

1 teaspoon ground cumin

½ teaspoon harissa paste

4 very large carrots, unpeeled

1 quart carrot juice

Fine sea salt and freshly ground white pepper

10 to 15 fresh cilantro leaves, thinly sliced

5 to 10 fresh mint leaves, thinly sliced

Extra-virgin olive oil

Harissa, a pepper paste from North Africa, has a complex spiciness that goes well with the sweetness of the carrot. Large carrots are important here because you want them to cook slowly and absorb all the juices and flavor from the broth.

PREHEAT THE OVEN TO 400°F.

In a large ovenproof sauté pan, heat the canola oil over medium-low heat. Add the garlic and shallot and sweat the vegetables until soft and translucent, about 2 minutes.

Stir in the cumin and harissa, then add the carrots, carrot juice, and salt and white pepper to taste. Increase the heat to bring the mixture to a high simmer.

Transfer the pan to the oven. Roast the carrots for 25 minutes, basting with the liquid every 5 minutes. Continue roasting, but without basting, until the carrots are tender at the thickest part (check with a paring knife), 5 to 10 minutes longer.

Remove from the oven and transfer the carrots to a serving bowl. Taste the liquid and adjust the seasoning if necessary. Pour the liquid and cooked garlic and shallots over the carrots, and garnish with the cilantro, mint, and a few drops of extra-virgin olive oil. Serve immediately.

ZUCCHINI PANCAKES

SERVES 4 (MAKES ABOUT 8 CAKES)

These savory pancakes are fun to make. They are light in texture but strong on zucchini flavor. I like them best when they are moist and fluffy. Serve immediately.

IN A SMALL BOWL, stir together the yogurt, dill, and salt and white pepper to taste. Cover and refrigerate until ready to serve the pancakes.

On the large holes of a box grater, grate the zucchini into a bowl. Combine the grated zucchini, onion, and a pinch of salt and gently toss. Set aside for 5 minutes.

Transfer the zucchini mixture to the center of a clean kitchen towel and squeeze out as much water as possible over a sink.

In a large bowl, whisk the eggs together. Add the zucchini mixture, cornmeal, baking powder, 1 teaspoon salt, and white pepper to taste and mix well.

In a large sauté pan, heat 1 tablespoon of the canola oil over medium heat. Add the batter to the pan by the heaping spoonful, to create cakes that are about 3 inches across. Cook them until golden brown on both sides, about 2 minutes per side. Transfer to a plate and keep warm. Repeat with the remaining canola oil and pancake batter.

Serve the pancakes hot with yogurt-dill sauce.

½ cup sheep's-milk yogurt

2 tablespoons finely chopped fresh dill

Fine sea salt and freshly ground white pepper

2 medium zucchini, stem ends trimmed off

¼ small red onion, diced

2 large eggs

½ cup fine cornmeal

1 teaspoon baking powder

3 tablespoons canola oil

SPECIAL EQUIPMENT
Box grater

VEGETABLE PANINI

SERVES 4

1 tablespoon canola oil

2 tomatoes, each cut horizontally into four ½-inch-thick slices

Fine sea salt and freshly ground white pepper

1 medium zucchini, sliced lengthwise into ⅛-inch-thick planks

1 yellow summer squash, sliced lengthwise into ⅛-inch-thick planks

1 medium eggplant, sliced lengthwise into ⅛-inch-thick planks

4 sandwich rolls (8 inches long)

½-pound ball fresh mozzarella cheese, cut into 8 equal slices

SPECIAL EQUIPMENT

Panini press or grill pan

Wire rack

I love this sandwich for the way the melted mozzarella oozes over the warm vegetables, and you get a good crunch of the bread when you take your first bite. If you don't have a panini press and you're using a grill pan, make sure you use a spatula to press down on the sandwich heavily and often throughout the process.

IN A LARGE SAUTÉ PAN, heat the canola oil over medium-high heat. Season the tomato slices with salt and white pepper. Sauté the tomato slices for 3 to 4 minutes, until soft, then transfer to a plate to cool.

Preheat a panini press (or a grill pan) to medium-high heat, making sure the cooking surface is very clean. Lightly season the zucchini, summer squash, and eggplant with salt and white pepper. Working in batches, grill the slices about 1 minute per side, transferring the cooked vegetables to a wire rack to cool.

Slice open the sandwich rolls and fill each with a layer of tomato, zucchini, summer squash, eggplant, and 2 slices of mozzarella. Close the sandwiches.

Cooking two at a time, place the sandwiches in the panini press and press the sandwiches for about 2 minutes per side (or cook on a grill pan, pressing down hard with a spatula). Keep warm and repeat with the remaining sandwiches. Slice in half and serve hot.

BRAISED LEEKS RAVIGOTE

SERVES 4 (MAKES ABOUT 1 CUP VINAIGRETTE)

Ravigote is a classic of French cuisine. The leeks must be cooked until tender—otherwise they will be stringy and unpleasant. The ravigote brings the right amount of richness and acidity to complement the flavor and texture of the leeks.

SET UP A LARGE BOWL of ice and water. In a large pot, bring 3 quarts of water to a boil, then add 1 teaspoon salt. Add the leeks and cook until softened, 6 to 8 minutes. Transfer to the ice bath to cool, then drain. Set aside.

Meanwhile, in a bowl, whisk together the vinegar, mustard, and a pinch of salt, then slowly whisk in the canola oil. Add the chopped egg, capers, shallot, cornichon, chives, tarragon, and parsley. Set the vinaigrette aside.

Place leek halves in the oven to reheat for 7 minutes or until just warm. Place two leek halves on each of four plates. Spoon vinaigrette over and around leeks, season with white pepper, and serve immediately.

Fine sea salt

4 medium leeks, green tops trimmed, halved lengthwise, and washed well

2 tablespoons aged sherry vinegar

1 tablespoon Dijon mustard

6 tablespoons canola oil

1 large hard-boiled egg, finely chopped

1 teaspoon finely chopped brined capers

1 teaspoon finely chopped shallot

1 teaspoon finely chopped cornichon

1 teaspoon finely chopped fresh chives

1 teaspoon finely chopped fresh tarragon

1 teaspoon finely chopped fresh parsley

Freshly ground white pepper

CARAMELIZED BRAISED ENDIVE

SERVES 4

6 heads Belgian endive,
outer leaves removed,
halved lengthwise

1 teaspoon sugar

Fine sea salt and freshly
ground white pepper

1 teaspoon canola oil

1 tablespoon unsalted butter

As a kid, I didn't enjoy endive too much because it was bitter. That bitterness has been lost over time and today it is pretty sweet when cooked until very tender and fully caramelized.

PREHEAT THE OVEN TO 400°F.

Season the cut sides of each endive half with the sugar and salt and white pepper to taste.

In a large ovenproof sauté pan, heat the canola oil over medium heat, then add the butter. Once the butter has foamed and subsided, add the endives, cut side down, and let them cook over medium heat until golden brown, 3 to 5 minutes.

Add a few tablespoons of water to cover the bottom of the pan, then transfer to the oven to roast until the endives are very tender, 15 to 17 minutes. Remove from the oven, taste, season if necessary, and serve hot.

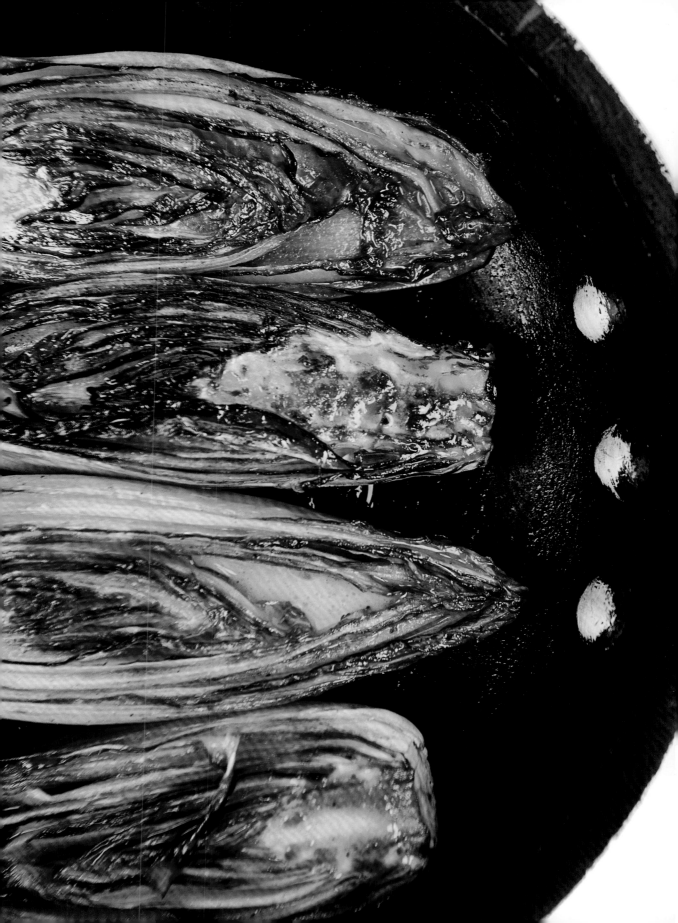

THE REAL RATATOUILLE

SERVES 4

In the South of France, everyone has a "real" ratatouille recipe, whether it be from their grandmother, mother, aunt, distant cousin, or friend of a friend of a friend. I've tasted many variations over the years. Some are made by cooking the vegetables separately and combining them at the end, though I don't find that necessary, as I love when the flavors of all the ingredients marry together while cooking. I do make sure to follow the right order for adding each vegetable to the pot, as the different textures require different cooking times.

IN A LARGE SAUTÉ PAN, heat the olive oil over medium heat. Add the onion, garlic, and bell pepper and sauté until tender, about 5 minutes.

Add the zucchini and eggplant, stir well, and cook for 5 minutes. Add the tomatoes and oregano and cook, stirring occasionally, until the vegetables are tender and the liquid has evaporated, 10 to 15 minutes. Season the mixture with salt and pepper and serve hot.

¼ cup extra-virgin olive oil

1 medium onion, cut into 1-inch chunks

3 garlic cloves, thinly sliced

1 red bell pepper, cut into 1-inch squares

2 small zucchini, cut into 1-inch cubes

1 medium eggplant, peeled and cut into 1-inch cubes

3 medium tomatoes, seeded and cut into 1-inch chunks

1 tablespoon fresh oregano leaves, finely chopped

Fine sea salt and freshly ground black pepper

POTATO TORTILLA ESPAÑOLA

SERVES 6

1 medium yellow onion, finely chopped

2 garlic cloves, finely chopped

Canola oil

1 pound Yukon Gold potatoes, peeled and sliced into ¼-inch-thick rounds (about 3 cups)

Fine sea salt and freshly ground white pepper

3 large eggs

Chef Frederico Ribeiro of New York City's Té Company's version of the Spanish potato omelet is an ethereal, gravity-defying miracle. You'll know you've succeeded when you cut into it and the egg is delicate and soft, moving just a little, while the potato filling stays in place. It's perfection.

IN A LARGE POT, combine the onion and garlic and add canola oil to cover the mixture by 1 inch. Cook over high heat until the mixture is sizzling, then reduce the heat to low and cook until the onions are translucent, about 10 minutes.

Season the potatoes generously with salt and white pepper, then transfer them to the pot with the onions and increase the heat, stirring the mixture until it comes to a simmer. Reduce the heat to low and cook until the potatoes are soft and creamy, about 15 minutes.

Drain the contents of the pot into a large sieve set over a bowl. Transfer the potato/onion mixture from the sieve to another bowl. Strain the oil, let cool, and reserve. Crack the eggs into the hot potato mixture and stir immediately, slightly breaking up the potatoes.

You will need a 6-inch nonstick sauté pan and a large flat plate that's slightly larger than the pan. Use warm water to rinse the plate, as this will help the *tortilla* slide back into the pan. Set the plate by the stove. Heat the pan over medium heat and add 2 tablespoons of the reserved oil. Add the egg and potato batter, swirling the pan to keep the batter from sticking to the sides. Cook just until the batter begins to set when the pan is swirled, no more than 2 minutes.

Remove the pan from the heat, cover with the plate, and carefully flip so that the *tortilla* is now on the plate, cooked side up. Add just enough of the reserved oil to coat the pan. Gently slide the *tortilla* back into the pan, reshaping it as necessary. Return the pan to the heat and cook the *tortilla* for 1 to 2 minutes to set. Remove the pan from the heat, let sit 1 minute, then slide the *tortilla* onto a clean plate. Let rest for a few minutes to set. Cut into wedges to serve.

EGGPLANT AU POIVRE

SERVES 4

The inspiration for this dish comes straight from my mother's steak au poivre, which she always made with filet mignon. The soft and meaty flesh of the eggplant mimics the texture of the filet and works so well with the green peppercorn sauce. Unlike a filet, the eggplant should be fully cooked.

USE THE TIP OF A SHARP KNIFE to score one surface of each eggplant "steak." The cuts should be about ¼ inch apart and about ⅛ inch deep. Season each with salt and white pepper and let rest for 5 minutes, then rub each eggplant surface with a halved garlic clove.

Line a sheet pan with paper towels. Heat a large sauté pan over medium heat and add 3 tablespoons of the canola oil. Add the eggplant slices to the pan, scored side down, and cook until golden brown on both sides and easily pierced with a paring knife, 2 to 3 minutes per side. Transfer to the paper towels to drain any excess oil, and keep warm.

Return the sauté pan to medium heat and add the remaining 1 tablespoon canola oil. Add the shallot, chopped garlic, green peppercorns, and black pepper. Reduce the heat to medium-low and sweat until the shallot is soft and translucent, about 2 minutes. Remove from the heat and carefully add the Cognac. Return the pan to the heat and cook over medium-high until the liquid is reduced by two-thirds. Add the cream and simmer until the sauce has thickened slightly and coats the back of a spoon, about 5 minutes. Taste the sauce with a clean spoon and season with salt.

Distribute the cooked eggplant slices among four plates. Generously spoon the sauce over the top of each and serve hot.

1 large eggplant, peeled and cut crosswise into eight 1-inch-thick steaks

Fine sea salt and freshly ground white pepper

2 garlic cloves, 1 halved and 1 finely chopped

4 tablespoons canola oil

1 tablespoon minced shallot (about ¼ medium)

1 tablespoon brined green peppercorns, chopped

½ tablespoon freshly ground black pepper

¼ cup Cognac

1 cup heavy cream

RÖSTI POTATOES

SERVES 4

1 pound russet potatoes, peeled

Fine sea salt and freshly ground white pepper

2 tablespoons canola oil

2 tablespoons unsalted butter, diced

SPECIAL EQUIPMENT

Box grater

There are few potato dishes tastier or better looking than this! The russet potatoes caramelize in butter and give the dish a gorgeous, warm golden color. You'll know it's perfect when it's crunchy on the outside and soft on the inside.

ON THE LARGE HOLES OF A BOX GRATER, grate the potatoes into a bowl. Season lightly with salt and white pepper.

Squeeze out the potatoes by the handful to remove as much of the liquid as possible, and transfer the dry potatoes to a clean bowl.

Heat an 8-inch nonstick sauté pan over medium-high heat and add the canola oil. Add the potatoes to the hot oil, using a fork to spread them out in an even layer. Distribute the diced butter evenly over the surface of the potatoes. Reduce the heat to medium and cook the potatoes until golden brown on the bottom, about 10 minutes.

Use a spatula to flip the rösti and cook until golden brown, another 6 to 8 minutes. Transfer the cooked rösti to a cutting board to rest for 5 minutes, then slice and serve.

CURRIED BRUSSELS SPROUTS

SERVES 4

Brussels sprouts taste best when they are glazed. The light heat of the Madras curry is an unexpected surprise and also adds a welcome burst of color. I like to quarter the sprouts to speed up the cooking process, but also because it them gives them a better texture, and they are easier to eat if bite-sized.

IN A LARGE SAUTÉ PAN, heat the oil over medium-high heat. Add the Brussels sprouts and season lightly with salt and white pepper. Reduce the heat to medium and sauté for 3 minutes. Add 3 tablespoons of water and the butter and cook until the water is reduced by half. Add the curry powder, tossing to evenly distribute. Cook until the water has evaporated and the Brussels sprouts are tender, 2 to 3 minutes. Add the lemon juice, adjust the seasoning if necessary, and serve hot.

1 teaspoon canola oil

1 pound Brussels sprouts, trimmed and quartered

Fine sea salt and freshly ground white pepper

1 tablespoon unsalted butter

1 tablespoon Madras curry powder

Juice of ½ lemon

SPINACH GRATIN

SERVES 4

4 tablespoons (½ stick) unsalted butter

½ medium onion, finely chopped

Fine sea salt

3 pounds baby spinach, chopped

1 cup heavy cream

1 cup panko bread crumbs

Freshly ground white pepper

SPECIAL EQUIPMENT

6 × 6-inch ceramic or glass baking dish

The bread crumbs bring a nice, crunchy contrast to the soft spinach and cream mix. This requires a good amount of spinach, as the spinach gives up a lot of water while cooking and shrinks substantially. Regular spinach can be substituted for baby spinach, but make sure to remove the large stems. I don't recommend frozen spinach, as I find it a little too leafy. Regular bread crumbs can be substituted for panko if you prefer.

PREHEAT THE OVEN TO 400°F.

In a large sauté pan, melt the butter over medium-low heat. Add the onion, season with salt, and sweat until translucent, about 5 minutes.

Adding the spinach in batches, cook over medium heat until it is wilted and the liquid has evaporated, about 5 minutes. Add the cream and cook until it is reduced by half, about 4 minutes. Remove from the heat and transfer the spinach mixture to a 6 × 6-inch baking dish.

Cover the spinach mixture with panko, season with white pepper, and bake until golden brown and bubbling, 30 to 35 minutes. Let rest for 10 minutes, then serve hot.

SOY-GLAZED RED CABBAGE

SERVES 4

As cabbage dishes go, this one is really exciting! It's a surprising combination of Western cooking with a touch of Asian flavor. Adding soy to the butter creates a gorgeous, shiny glaze that makes the marvelous color of the cabbage extra glossy. The aged sherry vinegar brings just the right amount of acidity.

IN A LARGE SAUTÉ PAN, bring ½ cup water and the butter to a simmer. Season each cabbage wedge with salt and white pepper and add to the pan, cover with foil, and cook for 20 minutes.

Flip the wedges over and cook until the water has evaporated and the cabbage is tender, about 15 minutes. Add the sherry vinegar, flipping the cabbage once more to coat. Cook until the vinegar is reduced by half.

Remove from the heat and, using a pastry brush, brush each wedge with soy sauce and let caramelize in the hot pan for 2 minutes. Serve immediately.

4 tablespoons (½ stick) unsalted butter

1 red cabbage, cut through the core into 8 wedges

Fine sea salt and freshly ground white pepper

2 tablespoons aged sherry vinegar

2 tablespoons soy sauce

SPECIAL EQUIPMENT

Pastry brush

CHOU FARÇI

SERVES 8

Fine sea salt

1 head Savoy cabbage, dark
outer leaves removed

2 tablespoons unsalted butter

½ medium onion, cut into
small dice

2 garlic cloves, finely chopped

1 large carrot, peeled and
cut into small dice

2 ribs celery, cut into small dice

1¼ pounds button mushrooms,
washed and finely chopped

1 bay leaf

Freshly ground white pepper

1 large egg, beaten

1 cup panko bread crumbs

There is an exception to every rule, and this recipe, contrary to the title of the book, isn't actually that simple. In fact, it requires quite a lot of attention. This classic French stuffed cabbage is a staple in the winter. Here, the obvious twist on the classic is that there is no meat. However, it's packed with flavor and making it comes with the added bonus of mastering a complex recipe—your guests will be dazzled!

IN A LARGE POT, bring 6 quarts of water to a boil and season with 1 tablespoon salt. Blanch the cabbage in the water for 20 minutes, then transfer to a colander over a sink to drain and cool.

Meanwhile, in a large sauté pan, melt the butter over medium-low heat. Add the onion and garlic. Sweat for 2 minutes, then stir in the carrot, celery, mushrooms, and bay leaf. Season with salt and white pepper, increase the heat to medium, and cook, stirring regularly, until the moisture from the mushrooms has evaporated, 12 to 15 minutes. Remove from the heat and let cool, then stir in the beaten egg and panko.

Preheat the oven to 350°F.

Place the cabbage upright on a cutting board, with the core in the middle of the board. Carefully open the leaves until you reach the heart of the cabbage, which should be about the size of an apple. Carefully detach the heart with a sharp knife, removing most of it but leaving the cabbage leaves attached. Using two-thirds of the mushroom mix, form a ball of filling and place it in the center of the cabbage where the heart used to be. Fold the next two layers of cabbage leaves over the center of the filling to re-create the shape of the cabbage. Using the remaining one-third of the filling, completely cover the already folded layers of leaves. Then fold the rest of the cabbage leaves over the mushroom filling one by one, making sure the leaves overlap tightly.

Transfer the cabbage to a shallow roasting pan and roast in the oven for 30 minutes. Remove from the oven. Using a metal skewer or a paring knife, pierce the cabbage, letting the skewer or knife rest inside for 10 seconds. Remove and check if the metal is hot. If so, cut into eighths and serve hot.

RUTABAGA GRATIN

SERVES 4

This gratin is similar to a traditional potato dauphinois, but with much less starch and a lighter consistency. I love the bittersweet turnip-like flavor of the rutabaga. You can use cheddar here instead of Gruyère for a similar effect.

PREHEAT THE OVEN TO 400°F.

In a medium saucepot, combine the cream, garlic, and thyme and bring to a simmer. Remove from the heat and let sit for 10 minutes, then strain and discard the solids.

Butter a 9 × 13-inch baking dish. Cover the bottom of the dish with a layer of rutabaga, season with salt and white pepper, and repeat until the baking dish has been filled. Pour the warm cream over the rutabaga and top with the Gruyère.

Place the baking dish on a baking sheet, transfer to the oven, and bake until the cheese is browned and the cream is bubbling, about 45 minutes. Remove from the oven and use a paring knife to pierce the gratin—there should be little resistance. Let rest for 30 minutes, then slice and serve.

1¼ cups heavy cream

2 garlic cloves, peeled

3 sprigs thyme

1 tablespoon unsalted butter, for the baking dish

2 pounds rutabaga, peeled and sliced on a mandoline into ⅛-inch-thick half-moons

Fine sea salt and freshly ground white pepper

1 cup grated Gruyère cheese (about 4 ounces)

SPECIAL EQUIPMENT

Mandoline

MATCHA PICK-ME-UP

SERVES 1

¼ cup filtered water

2 teaspoons matcha powder

When I'm tired and that afternoon slump takes over, I make this instead of reaching for coffee. I whisk matcha powder in hot water until it's smooth and slightly frothy. I discovered the best matcha during a trip to Japan, in the region between the Kyoto and Osaka prefectures. Good-quality matcha is essential, and I buy mine from Ippodo, the iconic Japanese teahouse in New York City.

SPECIAL EQUIPMENT

Matcha whisk or small wire whisk

IN A SMALL PAN, bring the water to a simmer. Remove from the heat and let stand 1 minute.

Sift the matcha powder into a bowl and add the water. Use a matcha whisk or small wire whisk to whip the mixture until foamy. Serve immediately.

FROSÉ

SERVES 4 TO 6

I couldn't help including a recipe for frosé, as it's so much fun to make and so easy to drink. Plus, what more do you want on a hot day? It's basically a rosé granita, so technically you can eat it with a spoon, but I serve it in martini glasses and drink as it melts. It's ideal for parties and summer entertaining.

1 bottle (750 ml) dry rosé wine

POUR THE ROSÉ INTO A 9 × 13-INCH BAKING PAN and place it in the freezer for 8 hours, scraping and breaking up the freezing wine once or twice while it sets.

After 8 hours, use a fork to scrape the frozen wine to create a shaved-ice texture. Spoon the frosé into chilled glasses and serve immediately.

SPICED MULLED WINE

SERVES 12

1 bottle (750 ml) Merlot wine

¼ cup port wine

2 tablespoons sugar

1 cinnamon stick

3 whole cloves

½ nutmeg, grated

4 allspice berries

½-inch cube fresh ginger, peeled

2-inch strip orange zest, removed with a vegetable peeler

Mulled wine is a holiday favorite of mine. The aroma, flavors, and warmth invoke so many happy memories of festive gatherings and ski trips with the family. This one warms you up and gives you a nice buzz. I love the complexities of the hot wine with the cinnamon, cloves, nutmeg, and spices.

IN A HEAVY-BOTTOMED POT, combine the wine, port, sugar, spices, ginger, and orange zest. Bring to a simmer and let simmer for 20 minutes.

Remove from the heat, cover, and let steep for 2 hours.

Strain and discard the solids and serve warm.

EVERYTHING SMOOTHIE

SERVES 4

Full credit goes to my wife, Sandra, for this recipe. It's called the Everything Smoothie because she really includes a bit of everything that she has squirreled away and put in the freezer, ready to be blitzed in the blender on any given morning. Fruit that is becoming too ripe gets diced and saved, as well as watery vegetables such as cucumbers and celery. It's a genius idea, as not only does it taste good, it reduces food waste. If it's too thick, thin it out with coconut water.

IN A BLENDER, combine the soy milk, berries, banana, apple, grapes, cucumber, and celery. Scoop in the avocado flesh. Puree until the mixture is smooth. Use coconut water to thin the smoothie to your desired texture. Serve immediately or store in the refrigerator.

½ cup soy milk

½ cup halved strawberries

½ cup blueberries

½ cup raspberries

1 banana, coarsely chopped

1 green apple,
coarsely chopped

½ cup seedless grapes

1 Persian (mini) cucumber,
coarsely chopped

1 rib celery, coarsely chopped

½ avocado, halved and pitted

Coconut water, as needed

SPECIAL EQUIPMENT
Blender

BAKED CANDIED APPLES

SERVES 4

4 Gala apples

½ cup sugar

2 tablespoons unsalted butter

1 vanilla bean

This is an easy recipe with a small challenge: ensuring that the apples don't break during the cooking process. When cooked, the warm, caramelized, glossy apples feature the same delicious flavors as a tarte Tatin but are a lot lighter, not to mention a lot simpler to make. They are wondrous on their own, but more often than not I add whipped cream or vanilla ice cream (or sometimes both). You can add toppings such as chopped nuts as well if you wish. These will never not be a hit.

SPECIAL EQUIPMENT

Apple corer

PREHEAT THE OVEN TO 400°F.

Cut ¼ inch off the top and bottom of each apple. Core the apples with apple corer and peel, but leave the apples whole.

Place a small sauté pan over medium heat. Sprinkle the sugar into the hot pan, 1 tablespoon at a time, and cook, stirring occasionally, until the sugar cooks into a medium-dark caramel, 8 to 10 minutes.

Add the butter, whisking together until the mixture is emulsified. Remove from the heat. Split the vanilla bean down one side using a paring knife. Scrape the vanilla seeds from the pod into the caramel.

Transfer the caramel to an 8 × 8-inch baking pan and tightly pack the apples directly on top of the caramel. Cover the pan with foil.

Transfer to the oven and bake for 1 hour and 20 minutes. Remove from the oven and turn the apples over. Re-cover with the foil and bake until a skewer easily pierces the apples, about another 20 minutes. Remove from the oven and let rest 30 minutes. Baste the apples with a little of the remaining caramel from the pan, then transfer to a plate and serve warm.

CORN CAKE, BLUEBERRY COMPOTE

SERVES 8

I am far from an expert pastry chef, because I like to impro-vise when I cook and have a hard time following specific directions. But on the rare occasion that I do bake, I try my best to be disciplined and precise about it, making sure all my measurements are exact and all the steps are followed care-fully. Therefore, I'm usually pretty happy with the result.

MAKE THE COMPOTE: In a small saucepan, combine half the blueber-ries, the sugar, and the lemon juice and bring to a boil, stirring frequently. Cook, continuing to stir, until the mixture is reduced by half, about 10 minutes. Remove from the heat, stir in the lemon zest, and let cool. Once cool, fold in the remaining blueberries.

Make the corn cake: Preheat the oven to 325°F. Use a pastry brush to butter an 8 × 4 × 2-inch loaf pan thoroughly with a thin coat. Dust with flour, then turn over, tap excess flour out, and set aside.

In a medium sauté pan, melt the 3 tablespoons butter and add the corn. Cook over medium heat until the corn is tender, 5 to 8 minutes.

Transfer the cooked corn to a food processor and puree until smooth. Add the sugar and eggs, puree until smooth, then add the sour cream, flour, and baking powder and puree to combine.

Scrape the batter into the prepared loaf pan and bake until a skewer comes out clean, about 25 to 30 minutes, rotating the pan front to back after 15 minutes.

Let the cake cool in the pan, slice, and serve with the compote on top.

COMPOTE

2 pints blueberries

½ cup sugar

Grated zest and juice of 1 lemon

CORN CAKE

Butter and flour for the pan

3 tablespoons unsalted butter

1 ear corn, shucked, kernels cut from cob

2¾ cups sugar

3 large eggs

1 cup sour cream

2½ cups all-purpose flour

2 teaspoons baking powder

SPECIAL EQUIPMENT

Pastry brush

Food processor

CHERRY CLAFOUTIS

SERVES 4 TO 6

½ tablespoon unsalted butter for the pan

1½ cups cherries, pitted

1½ cups heavy cream

3 large eggs

1 tablespoon vanilla paste or extract

⅓ cup sugar

½ cup all-purpose flour

¾ teaspoon salt

Late spring, when cherries are in season, is the best time to make clafoutis. My family in France would be deeply offended that I pit the cherries here, as the pit supposedly enhances the flavor of the cherries. I politely disagree! I don't taste much of a difference, if any, and it's much easier to eat without the pits.

PREHEAT THE OVEN TO 400°F. Butter a shallow 9 × 9-inch baking pan or a 7 × 11-inch baking dish.

Arrange the cherries on the bottom of the baking pan or dish in an even layer.

In a large bowl, whisk together the cream, eggs, and vanilla. Whisk in the sugar, flour, and salt until smooth.

Strain the batter through a fine-mesh sieve and carefully pour over the cherries. Bake until the custard is set and evenly browned, about 25 minutes. Let rest for 10 minutes and serve warm.

FROZEN ESPRESSO SOUFFLÉS

MAKES 6 SOUFFLÉS

I love to surprise dinner guests with this. It's a stunning dessert that will wow anyone you put it in front of, and the best part is that it's very easy to make. A real winner.

WRAP A STRIP OF PARCHMENT PAPER around the outside of each of six 3-inch-diameter ramekins or espresso cups, creating a 1½-inch collar rising above the rim. Secure the parchment with paper clips.

In a bowl, with an electric mixer, whip the cream to stiff peaks. Refrigerate.

In a small saucepan, melt the butter and chocolate over medium-low heat, whisking it gently to combine. Remove from the heat and set aside.

In a double boiler over simmering water, whisk together the sugar, egg yolks, and espresso powder until the sugar dissolves and the mixture becomes pale yellow and frothy, about 5 minutes. Transfer the mixture to the bowl of an electric mixer and whip on high speed until the mixture doubles in volume.

Working in two batches, fold the chocolate mixture into the egg mixture. Then, working in two batches, fold the whipped cream from the refrigerator into the chocolate/egg mixture.

Pour the mixture into the prepared ramekins or espresso cups. Place in the freezer until frozen, 6 to 8 hours.

Remove the soufflés from the freezer and garnish with chocolate shavings or cocoa powder. Remove the parchment collars and serve frozen.

1 quart heavy cream

1 tablespoon unsalted butter

2 ounces milk chocolate

1 cup sugar

8 egg yolks

2 teaspoons espresso powder

Chocolate shavings or cocoa powder, for garnish

SPECIAL EQUIPMENT

Parchment paper

Six 3-inch-diameter ramekins or espresso cups

Electric mixer

Double boiler

VEGETABLE SIMPLE

217

CARAMELIZED PINEAPPLE

SERVES 4

¾ cup sugar

1 cup rum

2 tablespoons vanilla paste or extract

1 pineapple, peeled, quartered, cored, and cut into 4-inch lengths

1 teaspoon Maldon sea salt

For the best results here, use a very ripe pineapple. You can tell how ripe it is if it's soft when you press on it and the color of the skin is pretty brown, with very little green. This means the fruit will be quite sweet, which is what you're looking for. I serve it warm or at room temperature, often with a scoop or two of vanilla ice cream.

PREHEAT THE OVEN TO 375°F.

In a saucepan, heat the sugar over medium-high heat, stirring regularly, to create a dark caramel, 10 to 12 minutes. Remove from the heat, add the rum, and stir in the vanilla. Return the pan to the stove, bring to a boil, and cook until reduced by half, about 5 minutes.

Arrange the pineapple in a baking pan and coat it all over with the rum caramel. Season with the salt.

Transfer to the oven and roast until well caramelized, about 30 minutes, basting the pineapple with the sauce every 10 minutes and rotating the pan front to back each time you baste. Let stand at room temperature for 10 minutes, then serve.

CARROT CAKE

SERVES 8

I first learned about carrot cake when I came to America. I thought it was a joke, but when I tried it for the first time and tasted all at once the sweetness, spiciness, and the creamy frosting, I was blown away. What a revelation! It's now one of my favorite cakes.

MAKE THE CREAM CHEESE FROSTING: In a stand mixer fitted with the paddle attachment, combine the cream cheese, powdered sugar, vanilla, and lemon zest and beat together until smooth. Refrigerate until ready to use.

Make the cake: Preheat the oven to 325°F. Butter and flour a 9-inch round cake pan.

In a medium bowl, whisk together the flour, the baking powder, baking soda, cinnamon, nutmeg, and ginger.

In a large bowl, stir together the oil and granulated sugar, then stir in the eggs. Add the carrots, raisins, and pineapple. Fold the flour mixture into the carrot mixture, mixing to thoroughly combine.

Pour the batter into the prepared pan. Bake until set in the center, 20 to 30 minutes. Remove from the oven and let cool to room temperature in the pan.

Remove the cake from the pan and top with the frosting. Cut into wedges and serve.

CREAM CHEESE FROSTING

4 ounces cream cheese, at room temperature

1 cup powdered sugar

½ tablespoon vanilla extract

Finely grated zest of ½ lemon

CAKE

Butter and flour for the pan

2 cups all-purpose flour

1 teaspoon baking powder

¾ teaspoon baking soda

2 teaspoons ground cinnamon

¼ teaspoon grated nutmeg

½ teaspoon ground ginger

1½ cups canola oil

2¼ cups granulated sugar

4 large eggs

3 cups grated carrots (about 3 large)

⅔ cup raisins

½ cup diced fresh pineapple

SPECIAL EQUIPMENT

Stand mixer

CHOCOLATE MOUSSE

SERVES 4

1 cup dark chocolate chips (70% cacao)

1⅔ cups heavy cream

2 teaspoons vanilla extract

¼ teaspoon fine sea salt

4 egg whites

½ cup sugar

Cocoa powder, for garnish

SPECIAL EQUIPMENT

Double boiler

Thermometer

Electric mixer

They say 60 percent of your body is made up of water, however I'm sure mine is 60 percent chocolate mousse! I ate it almost daily in my formative years, with no regrets. It is one of the most (if not *the* most) satisfying ways to appreciate chocolate. I just love the silky texture combined with the powerful but not-too-rich flavor. I recommend 70% cacao, but if you are a dark chocolate superfan, you can go as high as 85%. It won't be as sweet and will carry some bitterness, but it will maintain the same consistency.

IN A DOUBLE BOILER over simmering water, melt the chocolate and transfer to a large bowl. Set aside to cool to 90°F.

Meanwhile, in a bowl, with an electric mixer, whip the cream, vanilla, and salt until stiff peaks form. Transfer to another bowl and keep cold. In a clean bowl, whip the egg whites with the sugar until stiff peaks form. Set aside.

When the chocolate has cooled to 90°F, slowly fold half the egg whites into the melted chocolate, then repeat with half the whipped cream. Repeat with remaining egg whites then whipped cream until fully incorporated. Refrigerate the mousse to chill.

To serve, divide chocolate mousse among four chilled cups and garnish with cocoa powder.

STICKY TOFFEE PUDDINGS

SERVES 6

I discovered this marvelous dessert in New York City in the late '90s at a restaurant called Etats-Unis. Run by a father and son, it was a tiny place that seated sixteen people, max. You ordered dessert at the beginning, as they would make these little puddings to perfection à la minute. After I tasted it, I vowed to make this one of the few desserts in my repertoire.

MAKE THE PUDDINGS: Preheat the oven to 325°F.

In a small saucepot, combine the dates and enough water to just cover them. Bring to a boil, then remove from the heat, transfer to a blender, and puree until smooth.

In a bowl, combine the hot date puree with 8 tablespoons butter and the chocolate. Add the brown sugar and eggs and stir to combine.

In a separate bowl, whisk together the flour, baking soda, baking powder, and salt. Add the flour mixture to the date mixture and stir until just combined.

Grease the ramekins with the remaining tablespoon of butter. Place them on a baking sheet and divide the batter among them. Bake 20 to 25 minutes.

Make the sauce: In a medium saucepan, combine the brown sugar and butter and bring to a boil. Cook, stirring regularly, until the mixture is medium-dark brown.

Remove from the heat and slowly add the whiskey. Stir in the cream, vanilla, and orange zest and return to the heat. Bring to a boil and cook for 5 to 6 minutes, until the liquid is reduced by half.

To serve, invert the ramekins to slowly release the puddings onto individual plates. Pour the warm sauce over the top and serve.

PUDDINGS

9 tablespoons unsalted butter, at room temperature

2 cups chopped pitted dates

2 tablespoons finely chopped dark chocolate

¾ cup packed light brown sugar

2 large eggs

1¾ cups all-purpose flour

¾ teaspoon baking soda

½ teaspoon baking powder

½ teaspoon salt

SAUCE

1½ cups packed light brown sugar

4 tablespoons (½ stick) unsalted butter

⅔ cup whiskey

2½ cups heavy cream

2 tablespoons vanilla paste or extract

Finely grated zest of ½ orange

SPECIAL EQUIPMENT

Six 3-inch ramekins

TIPS & GUIDELINES

A condensed guide to buying, storing, and making the most out of vegetables

1. SEASONS

There are reasons for the seasons! Fruits and vegetables purchased in their season will look, feel, smell, and taste their very best compared with those purchased out of season, even if only by a few weeks. For example, tomatoes are at their peak in summer because they require a lot of sunlight as well as a warm climate. Even when grown in the best artificial conditions, they won't be nearly as good as they are in the summer months. I encourage you to shop at farmers' markets whenever you can, as they are the best indication of what's in season.

2. ORGANIC

If you have the means and access, I recommend buying organic when possible. While organic produce is a little more expensive, it's a positive commitment to your health as well as the health of the environment. Organic fruits and vegetables are non-GMO and have not been treated with harmful pesticides or fertilizers that are potentially damaging to our land and waters. Buying organic doesn't necessarily guarantee the products will taste better, but the odds are higher that they will.

3. LOCAL

There are many benefits to buying local, whether directly from farmers or in stores that advocate for small food producers in the area. Supporting local growers is not only a great way to connect with farmers and artisans but supports the local economy, champions good food practices, and helps preserve land from large developments.

4. SHOPPING WITH YOUR SENSES

The trick to choosing the best produce at the market or grocery store is actually by taking a very logical approach to shopping. Once you pick a fruit or vegetable that's in season, use your senses to help you figure out which one is best. Your eyes give you a lot of information; you can see any damage, bruising, discoloration, and mold, as well as some signs of dryness or ripeness. Touching the item supports what you see; for instance, an avocado shouldn't be hard as a rock or too soft to the touch. And then there's your sense of smell, which is more instinctive. Good mushrooms have a very strong, fresh earthy smell; melons are sweet and slightly floral; and fennel is very aromatic—bright, sweet with strong hints of anise. These smells will stay with you, and the more you incorporate using your nose, the more you will develop your knowledge of what good produce smells like. Using your senses and your gut instincts, as well as the knowledge of what's in season, will result in a successful shopping trip.

5. TIMING / PLANNING + BUYING ONLY WHAT YOU NEED

It's important not to buy your produce too far in advance of when you plan to cook it, especially if you are close to the source. Once harvested, fruits and vegetables can be very sensitive to their new environment. Factors such as inadequate light, temperature, and storage conditions can speed up the deterioration process, so knowing when to buy will help reduce food waste. For example, greens and leafy salads lose their quality very quickly; however, a root vegetable can last much longer in the refrigerator before it starts to deteriorate. Meal planning is the key to not overpurchasing. I recommend shopping for fresh fruits and vegetables no longer than 48 hours in advance to avoid potential spoilage and to ensure you cook and eat your produce while it is still at its best. This practice saves money, lessens waste, and also limits the possibility of a repetitive diet.

6. STORAGE

Food storage can sometimes be an afterthought, but knowing some general rules of thumb will improve the shelf life of both your fresh and dried goods. Overall, root vegetables can be stored in a cool environment for a relatively long period of time. More sensitive vegetables, such as leafy greens and mushrooms, have a much shorter lifespan and can only be kept refrigerated for short periods of time. Produce such as melons and tomatoes actually lose their flavor if kept chilled, so are better off in a moderately temperate area of your kitchen or pantry. When storing fruits or vegetables, either in the refrigerator or in a dedicated area or cupboard in your kitchen, it's important not to stack them on top of each other, as some are more fragile than others. Aromatic foods should always be kept separate to avoid absorption by other foods—for example, garlic or an onion if it's been halved or peeled. Pastas, legumes (such as lentils and beans), and grains should be stored in airtight containers in a dark and dry place.

7. WASHING + CLEANING

More often than not, produce in the grocery store or market has been touched by many hands and it's almost always the case that fruits, vegetables, and fresh herbs have some residual dirt, soil, dusts, and sometimes insects from when they were harvested. Cleaning your produce before cooking helps avoid cross-contamination, removes impurities, as well as eliminates any nasty tastes and textures. When washing salad, pat dry with paper towels to remove excess water. Sometimes I find that water isn't enough, so I add a few drops of white vinegar when I'm cleaning fresh produce.

8. FREEZING

The main benefit of frozen food is that it can be kept for very long periods of time. I have found, with some exceptions, that it's almost always better to buy great-quality frozen vegetables than mediocre fresh equivalents. Vegetables destined to be frozen are harvested at their peak, and with the advances in technology and food preservation, it's very often the case that their nutrients are also preserved. Not every frozen vegetable is a good substitute for fresh, though, and nothing beats great-quality fresh produce.

9. LEFTOVERS, CUTTINGS + SCRAPS

Scraps and leftover cuttings (seeds, skins, peelings, and roots) can be composted or, depending on the condition and amount, added to other items to make stock for some soup and sauce bases. Remnants such as the last few berries, the final rib of celery, or a banana that's almost overripe can be frozen and used at a later stage for recipes such as the Everything Smoothie (page 209). And of course, leftovers for most, if not all of these recipes can be eaten at your next meal or the following day.

10. HAVE FUN!

Shopping for your ingredients should be an enjoyable experience. It's a way to disconnect from the rest of the day. It's also a great opportunity to get to know your local purveyors, farmers, and grocery store workers and develop a relationship with them. With a positive mind, trips to the market can be as rewarding and pleasurable as cooking and eating.

SEASONAL PRODUCE GUIDE

This list of seasonal produce is a guide to help navigate shopping for fruits and vegetables. Although today you can often find that many fruits and vegetables are available year-round, I want to highlight when they are at their peak seasons and most flavorful. This chart primarily pertains to produce grown in the Northern Hemisphere, which in most regions has four distinct seasons.

FALL

Apples	Corn	Pomegranate
Beets	Cremini mushrooms	Porcini mushrooms
Bell peppers	Cucumbers	Portobello mushrooms
Bok choy	Daikon	Pumpkin
Broccoli	Delicata squash	Radicchio
Broccoli rabe	Eggplant	Romaine lettuce
Brussels sprouts	Endive	Rutabaga
Butter lettuce	Fennel	Sage
Butternut squash	Garlic	Shallots
Button mushrooms	Horseradish	Shiitake mushrooms
Cabbage	Kale	Snow peas
Carrots	Leeks	Spinach
Cauliflower	Lentils	Sweet potatoes
Celery	Maitake mushrooms	Swiss chard
Celery root	Onions	Tomatoes
Chanterelles	Parsnips	Turnips
Chard	Pears	White truffles
Coconut	Persimmon	

WINTER

Apples

Bananas

Black truffles

Broccoli

Brussels sprouts

Butternut squash

Button mushrooms

Cabbage

Cauliflower

Celery

Celery root

Chicory

Coconut

Cranberries

Cremini mushrooms

Daikon

Escarole

Fennel

Grapefruit

Jerusalem artichokes/
sunchokes

Leeks

Lentils

Oranges

Parsnips

Pineapple

Plantains

Potatoes

Radicchio

Rosemary

Rutabaga

Sweet potatoes

Turnips

White beans

SPRING

Artichokes

Arugula

Asparagus

Avocados

Blueberries

Butter lettuce

Button mushrooms

Carrots

Cauliflower

Celery

Celery root

Chanterelle mushrooms

Chives

Cilantro

Cucumbers

Dill

Endive

Fava beans

Fennel

Garlic

Leeks

Limes

Mint

Morel mushrooms

Onions

Pea shoots

Peas

Radishes

Ramps

Rhubarb

Romaine lettuce

Rutabaga

Sage

Scallions

Shiitake mushrooms

Snow peas

Sugar snap peas

Sorrel

Spinach

Strawberries

Swiss chard

SUMMER

Avocados

Basil

Beets

Bell peppers

Blackberries

Blueberries

Bok choy

Butter lettuce

Button mushrooms

Carrots

Celery

Chanterelle mushrooms

Chard

Cherries

Chickpeas

Cilantro

Corn

Cucumbers

Dill

Eggplant

Garlic

Green beans

Horseradish

Limes

Marjoram

Melons

Mint

Onions

Peaches

Peas

Plums

Porcini mushrooms

Potatoes

Radishes

Romaine lettuce

Shallots

Shishito peppers

Strawberries

Tarragon

Thyme

Tomatoes

Watermelon

Yellow squash

Zucchini

Zucchini blossoms

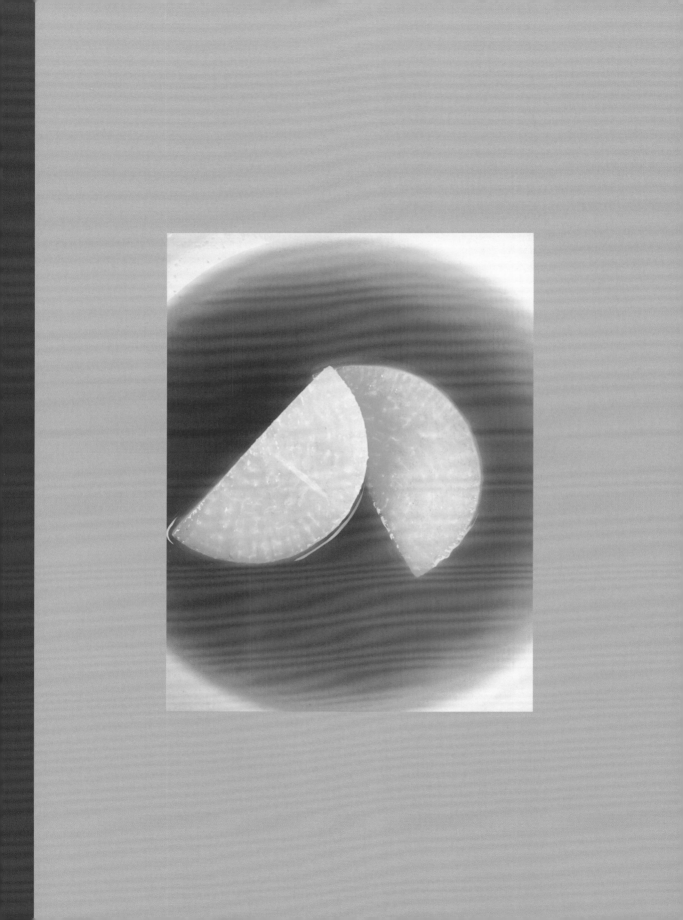

ACKNOWLEDGMENTS

Vegetable Simple was a long time in the making, from when I first conceived the idea to now, writing this note of gratitude. It became a very personal endeavor, and my passion for the book only increased throughout the process, and I am so glad to be able to finally share it with all of you. The reality of *Vegetable Simple* was only made possible by my close community of family, friends, and colleagues who believed in it and supported me over the few years it took to achieve.

Kim Witherspoon, my agent, champion, ally, but most important, my friend, who always strives for the best for me. Andy Ward for his trust and confidence in me as well as the entire Random House team for bringing this book to life. I would like to express a special appreciation to Susan Kamil, who sadly passed as I sat down to write this. Her support over the years meant so much and I, like many others, was blessed to have her in my corner.

My dear friend Nigel Parry, who took a chance, humored my crazy idea, and agreed to shoot this book. He captured these vegetables with the same passion and artistry as he does his portrait subjects.

My Le Bernardin family, to whom I'm indebted for their constant support and hard work and for allowing me the time needed to create this book. Special thanks to chef Erik Fricker with help from Tim Alvarez, and to our pastry chef Thomas Raquel, who worked tirelessly on the recipes, and to Laurie Woolever for testing, adapting, and formatting them. It took time and patience, for which I'm grateful.

Cathy Sheary, my professional guardian angel, who also collaborated with me in the writing process and persevered in project-managing the book from the beginning. Thanks also to Remy Albert for all her help at the final hurdles.

My wife, Sandra, and son, Adrien, for their unconditional love and support, and for being my biggest and best defenders. I love you both more every day.

To Maguy Le Coze for her unwavering friendship, encouragement, and belief in me.

Lastly, I would like to thank Matthieu Ricard, who, through his book *A Plea for the Animals*, planted the seed that ultimately led me to create *Vegetable Simple*.

INDEX

ABOUT THE AUTHOR

ERIC RIPERT is the chef and co-owner of the New York restaurant Le Bernardin, which holds three Michelin stars and has maintained a four-star rating from *The New York Times* for more than two decades. He is vice chairman of the board of City Harvest, a New York–based food rescue organization, as well as a recipient of the Légion d'Honneur, France's highest honor. He serves as a regular guest judge on Bravo's *Top Chef* and is the host of his own TV series, *Avec Eric*, which has won Emmy and James Beard awards. Ripert is the author of five cookbooks: *My Best: Eric Ripert, Avec Eric, On the Line, A Return to Cooking*, and *Le Bernardin: Four-Star Simplicity*, as well as a *New York Times* bestselling memoir, *32 Yolks*.

Facebook.com/chefericripert
Twitter: @ericripert
Instagram: @ericripert

8